DANIEL: MAN OF DESIRES

DANIEL: MAN OF DESIRES

By

DOM HUBERT VAN ZELLER

One thing have I desired of the Lord, and
this will I seek : that I may dwell in the
house of the Lord all the days of my life.

Psalm xxvi, 4.

THE NEWMAN PRESS • WESTMINSTER, MARYLAND

1951

First Published, 1940
Reprinted by The Newman Press, 1951

NIHIL OBSTAT:
Dom Richard Davey, O.S.B.,
Censor deputatus.

IMPRIMI POTEST:
W. E. Kelly, O.S.B.,
Ab. Pres.

NIHIL OBSTAT:
Censor deputatus.

IMPRIMATUR:
E. Morrogh Bernard,
Vic. Gen.

Westmonasterii,
die 10a Julii 1939.

Printed in the U. S. A.

TO

FATHER JOHN TALBOT

From the beginning of thy prayers the word came forth ; and I am come to show it to thee, because thou art a man of desires.

Daniel ix, 23.

And he said to me : Daniel, thou man of desires, understand the words that I speak to thee, and stand upright.

Daniel x, 11.

Therefore he that looked like a man touched me again and said to me, strengthening me : Fear not, O man of desires, peace be to thee : take courage and be strong. And when he spoke to me I grew strong.

Daniel x, 18, 19.

CONTENTS

CHRONOLOGICAL TABLE

626 B.C.   Nabopolassar, king of Babylon.
608   Death of Josias.
606 ?   Daniel taken to Babylon.
604   Nabuchodonosor, king of Babylon.
597   Joakin taken to Babylon.
586   Fall of Jerusalem.
561   Evil-Merodach, king of Babylon.
559   Neriglissar, king of Babylon.
556   Labashi-Marduk, king of Babylon.
555   Nabonidus, king of Babylon.
538   Fall of Babylon and death of Baltassar.
530   Death of Cyrus.
522   Death of Cambyses.

INTRODUCTION

I HAVE taken the incidents in the story of Daniel's life one by one as they appear in the text ; critics are found to follow a different order, but as I am not writing for the critics I thought it would be more convenient to adopt the existing sequence for the benefit of those who have the open Bible in front of them. Now even the most superficial reading of the Sacred Text will reveal the fact that there is no attempt at chronological sequence. On examination a plan suggests itself, but it is not a chronological one. The Book is seen to be divided into three clearly defined sections. The first six chapters (though scrappy and difficult to locate exactly) are chiefly concerned with historical facts ; the next six chapters are strictly prophetical ; the remaining two (which are tacked on almost as an afterthought) are not so much historical as personal and biographical. These last add nothing to antiquity or to prophecy, but form a supplement to the first part of the Book and are concerned with giving a number of episodes to which it is exceedingly difficult to put a date. The Protestant Bible ignores this section altogether ; it is not found in the Hebrew and owes its place at the end of the Book of Daniel instead of at the beginning (where it originally was) to St Jerome, who seems to have been considerably puzzled by it.

It will be noticed that I deal fairly fully with the first and third, but not at all with the middle section. Seven of the Prophet's fourteen chapters are thus passed over in silence. The reason for this is that the chapters omitted (with the exception of the thirteenth, the Susanna chapter, which will be referred to in a moment) have about them—as have the first six—a completeness which deserves a treatise to themselves. Such a treatise I am far from competent, or inclined, to write. In embarking upon the third part of Daniel's Book (the 'personal and biographical' appendix) I must further excuse myself because of the two chapters covered by the text I propose to leave out one—the Susanna chapter. It is not a sense of delicacy that urges me to draw the veil over this well-known episode so much as a feeling that really there is very little more that I can add. Chapter xiii is a complete short story in itself, and for any biographer of Daniel's to touch it up would be to rob it of its conciseness and therefore of half of its charm. I am quite aware that the exercise of selection, however discreet, is, in a biographer, a sin of the first magnitude, but since I claim to mix with Daniel many other things besides biographical details, why should I not reserve to myself equally the right to leave out some of them ?

I would remind the reader that dispute still rages over the authorship of Daniel. A very good case can be made for the theory that the Book is the work of two different people—neither of them being Daniel ! Certainly the objections to a single authorship are very telling. The oldest texts, for instance, give three different languages (Hebrew, Chaldaic, Greek) ; sudden changes occur from the third to the first person (making one wonder whether the author *can* be as absent-minded as all that !) ; and—to mention but one more of the many objections that are advanced—there is the width of knowledge with regard to contemporary civilisation possessed by the writer ; this knowledge is hardly to be attributed (apparently) to one of Daniel's limited, though variegated, outlook. In spite of the difficulties, however, no undue strain is being put upon the data when we choose to identify the author of the biography with the central figure. I, at any rate, have taken the authorship question for granted. Let him do otherwise who will. The Church has not pronounced.

Since the quotations from the Book of Daniel appear for the most part in their textual sequence I have not thought it necessary to give references ; the appropriate chapter in Daniel is cited at the head of those studies that rely chiefly on the Scripture text itself.

I express here my gratitude to all those who have, either in their written works or spoken words, assisted me in this representation of Daniel. In connexion with the help I have received from written works, it will perhaps be urged that the Bibliography which is printed at the end is somewhat jejune, and that I would have done better had I sought more help than in fact I have received. I know. The Bibliography at the end is far from adequate. But most of the English Protestant commentaries are out of print, and there are no Catholic commentaries in English at all. Should this book do no more than encourage people to take an interest in the Prophecy of Daniel (if only to tell me how much they dislike what I have said about it) I shall not deem my labours a waste of time.

Every word I write is submitted without reserve or qualification to the judgement of ecclesiastical authority in accordance with the wishes of the Holy See.

DOWNSIDE ABBEY,

DANIEL: MAN OF DESIRES

CHAPTER I

JUDA AT THE TIME OF DANIEL'S BIRTH

i

THE first we hear of Daniel is that he was led captive to Babylon in the ' third year of Joakim king of Juda.' Daniel's deportation, then, anticipated the series of deportations which constituted the Captivity by a matter of some twenty years. Jerusalem was not to yield finally to the power of Babylon until 586 B.C., and the ' third year of Joakim ' can hardly have been later than 606. The events which led up to the exile of Daniel will be briefly given below ; let us first of all consider the date of the Prophet's birth.

If 606 B.C. saw Daniel in Babylon, and if (as we learn from *v.* 4 of his opening chapter) he was already at that time ' skilful in wisdom, acute in knowledge, and instructed in science,' then the date of his birth must be somewhere in the region of 624 ; it is unlikely that he should have attained to such dizzy heights of learning before the age of seventeen at the earliest. This means that Daniel must have enjoyed about fourteen years of Josias's reign before witnessing the successive accessions of Joachaz and Joakim.

Josias was the last of Juda's kings to attempt—on anything like a large scale—a return to the Law of God.

It was this king who, with Jeremias at his elbow, had spent most of his long reign pulling down ' groves ' and clearing away ' shrines.'¹ Josias died (dramatically, and, as far as we can see, needlessly) at the battle of Mageddo in 609 ; it was to Egypt and not to Assyria or Chaldea that Juda yielded her independence on this occasion.² Josias was followed on the throne by his second son, Joachaz, who was replaced six months later by the elder brother Joakim. Both these sovereigns advocated a reversal of their father's reforming policies : idolatry and licence returned to Juda. During the three years between Josias's death and Daniel's exile a great deal—apart from the swift replacements upon the throne of Juda—took place in Palestine. In the first instance, Assyria crumbled away altogether ; secondly, Egypt was ousted from the lands it had succeeded in annexing ; and thirdly, Chaldea took over the territory and vassal states that had recently comprised the Assyrian Empire. Thus when we read that Daniel was carried away captive as a result of Joakim's ' rebellion,' it was not against the original overlords of Juda that the king was setting himself, nor yet against those to whom Juda was responsible in Joachaz's reign—namely, the Egyptians —it was the yoke of Babylon to which Joakim (unwisely)

¹ It is interesting to note that even the great prophet Isaias had not managed to do what between them Jeremias and Josias brought about ; Isaias, for example, had never succeeded in getting rid of the temple that Solomon had put up to the Moabite goddess, Chamos. This place of worship had stood on Mount Olivet—of all places—in full view of Jerusalem. Josias was responsible for its abolition.

² ' Semi-independence ' would perhaps be a better word, because Juda was still paying tribute to Nineveh. The Assyrian Empire, however, was decaying so rapidly that the practical freedom of Juda at this time was more or less assured. The date of Nineveh's fall is uncertain.

objected. Daniel owed his removal from Jerusalem to
Nabuchodonosor, the coadjutor king of the Chaldeans
and general of his father's, Nabopolassar's, armies.
We shall have a great deal to say about Nabuchodonosor later on, suffice to note here that having
assured himself that Joakim's abortive rebellion was
nothing very much to worry about he devoted himself
to other and more troublous frontiers. Nabopolassar,
the founder of the Neo-Babylonian Empire, died soon
after this (604), leaving Nabuchodonosor in sole
possession of the kingdom. By this time Daniel, of
course, has passed out of the history of Jerusalem and
is contributing generously to the history of the exiled
Jews in Babylon. I need only say further that Joakim
died in 597 and was succeeded by his son Joakin ;
Joakin reigned for six months and was then deposed
by Nabuchodonosor who was beginning to lose patience
with Juda's continued disaffection and double-dealing.
News of these many changes and disturbances would
have reached Daniel as he was trying to get used to the
manners of those with whom he was to spend the rest
of his days. He would have heard how Nabuchodonosor
had stripped the Temple of its ornaments, how he had
seized the person of the prophet Ezechiel (who was
even now on his way, in chains, to Tel-Abib in
Babylonia), how he had turned out of the Holy
City the principal tradesmen, craftsmen, officers, and
nobles. . . .

But the final humiliation of Jerusalem was not to be
for another ten years.

In the place of Joakin, Nabuchodonosor set
Mathanias upon the throne of Juda. Mathanias was
Josias's youngest son ; his name was changed by the
Babylonian to Sedecias. To cut a long story short,

Sedecias was every bit as unsatisfactory as his three predecessors had been : he was no use either to Juda or to Babylon. In 586 B.C., with the fall of Jerusalem, he ended his inglorious career as king, and so brought to an end the line of Juda's kings. Blinded, bound, and bereft of his two sons who had been executed at Reblatha, Sedecias followed his brothers and his nephew along the road that led to Babylon and to exile. The kingcraft of Israel had not been a success.

But to return to Daniel.

The boyhood, then, and the early manhood of the Prophet who is to be the subject of this biography must have been a veritable switch-back of educational and political experience. Both at home and in exile Daniel would have had to adjust himself to new loyalties at intervals of every few years—or even months. It is true that in the first years of his schooling Josias was alive (which meant that the Law was being taught in all the class- and lecture-rooms of Juda), but as soon as he was fourteen or so the Prophet's studies would have been cast incontinently into the melting-pot. Joachaz and Joakim were not men who looked with any kindly eye upon the study of theology.

During Daniel's Jerusalem period there were no less than three inspired prophets in Juda : Ezechiel, Sophonias, and (as we have seen) Jeremias.[1] If the prophecies contained in the middle section of Daniel's Book are anything to go by, it looks as though of the three it was the last-named—Jeremias—who influenced

---

[1] It is possible that Sophonias was dead by this time ; in which case perhaps the number can be made up by adding the name of Holda, the prophetess who advised Josias about the Book of the Law. Or, if Holda be objected to, there is Jeremias's secretary, Baruch (though this prophet was not to begin his career as prophet for some years to come).

our Prophet the most. It is thought by some, in fact, that Daniel was a pupil of the older prophet ; this seems to me hardly likely because of the ill-favour with which Jeremias was regarded by the teaching body in Jerusalem at the time ; also—and this is perhaps a better reason because a practical one—Jeremias was mostly employed during Josias's reign in wandering from town to town as an itinerant preacher of the newly discovered Book of Deuteronomy. Nor does it appear to me probable that Daniel was instructed by either Ezechiel or Sophonias : the work of the former bears little resemblance to Daniel's writing, while the latter was more of a court chaplain than an expounder of Sacred Scripture.

But whether or not the two servants of God, Daniel and Jeremias, were personally acquainted it is more than likely that the boy student would have gazed with reverence and awe at the preacher prophet. Daniel would have been familiar, and in sympathy with, the reforming activities of the famous Jeremias. It is not difficult to imagine a small hero-worshipper following with the wide eyes of wonder the footsteps of a gaunt ascetic who, with pages of manuscript under his arm, is striding from the Temple to the Court . . . ' Off on another missionary journey,' says Daniel to himself.

Then, after the calamity of Mageddo and with the new king Joachaz on the throne, Daniel would have had to adapt himself to quite a new order of things : his studies would have been altered, his oath of allegiance—first made when he was twelve years old— renewed in favour of Egypt instead of, as hitherto, to Assyria . . .

But as Juda had fallen before Egypt, Egypt was in its

turn to fall before Chaldea—and Daniel became a Babylonian subject. Which brings us back to 'the third year of Joakim' when that king 'rebelled,' and when Daniel was carried away captive with 'the vessels of the house of God.' Why, we ask, was Daniel chosen out for this exile when most of the nobles—removed, it is true, at a subsequent date— were allowed to remain at home in their heavily taxed capital ? The third verse of Daniel's first chapter tells us all about it.

> ' The king [Nabuchodonosor] spoke to Asphenez the master of the eunuchs that he should bring in some of the children of Israel and of the king's seed and of the princes, children in whom there was no blemish, well favoured and skilful in all wisdom, acute in knowledge and instructed in science, and such as might stand in the king's palace that he might teach them the learning and the tongue of the Chaldeans.'

So Daniel was chosen for three things : his looks, his learning, and his pedigree. Nabuchodonosor evidently wanted to parade the fruit of his Judean campaign on his return to the Chaldean capital. Not content with filling his sanctuaries with Hebrew plate, he wished the Babylonians to appreciate the human spoils of war. A few really presentable specimens of Jewish culture would convince his own, rather upstart, people that they had much to learn from the manners of other nations. We can feel for Daniel on his journey from the Holy City to Babylon ; his three qualifications would have seemed more in the nature of liabilities than assets. The ' comely appearance ' would have

made him the subject of jokes not always in the best
of taste ; the theological training he had received
would have been something to look back upon as one
of the many interrupted happenings that go to make
the pain of home-sickness ; while the comfortable
circumstances of his upbringing would have caused
him to shrink, in spite of himself, from the uncouth
manners of his escort and from the unaccustomed
trials of the road. No, it is not always an advantage
to be—what for want of a better term we must call—
a ' gentleman.'[1] If desert travel is at all conducive
to reflexion then Daniel's mind must have dwelt upon
subjects that are mostly not dealt with in the school-
room. Had we joined the caravan of youthful exiles
as it swayed and bumped along the dusty road from
Jerusalem to Babylon we should probably have found
it composed of about as miserable a party as had
ever crossed the Syrian Desert. Whatever the hopes
and ambitions of him who was afterwards to be called
the ' man of desires '[2] there can have been little enough

---

[1] Josephus infers from the reference to ' the king's seed ' and
the ' princes ' that the four young men who were selected by
Asphenez were related to King Sedecias. If this was so then for
Nabuchodonosor to turn them into court pages at Babylon was not
such a slight upon the subject nation as one might think at first
sight. The plundering of Jerusalem, however, was quite a different
matter. Esdras, writing many years later (after the ' return '),
seems to be profoundly impressed by the amount of valuables he
is able to bring back to the Holy City ' of all that Nabuchodonosor
had carried away as booty.' So, allowing for the loss between the
two journeys, the caravan load must, in the first instance, have
presented an appearance of splendour worthy of the Arabian Nights.
But it was not a splendour that redounded to the honour of the
captives : it was the spoil of war and not the dowry of rank.

[2] ix, 23 ; x, ii ; x, 19. I must here anticipate the critic who will
tell me that the Hebrew does not convey the meaning ' man of
desires,' but that ' man desired ' (or ' desirable man ') is nearer to
the original. I know. But since the idiom has been given to us
(through the Latin) in the form ' man of desires,' I am not bothering
myself, in a work of this kind, by the distinction.

in prospect to justify the slenderest expectation. To
Daniel it must have seemed that his desires had been
cut off in the bud. One wonders whether he had as yet
reached that stage in the soul's progress when every
desire is covered by the one desire—that of doing the
will of God. It is the stage where the wish is exchanged
for what is calmly chosen in the will. A step is felt
to be reached in the business of mounting towards God,
and it is a step which no one else can take for us—
except in the very rare cases when God Himself seems
to get tired of waiting, and does the thing on His
own account. Henry Suso, on this showing, is the
exception when he tells us that one day, standing before
a certain altar, he was suddenly stripped of every
wish and preference, and that from that time onwards
he was able to work the work of God. But even here,
of course, and in similar cases, the operation is found
to presuppose a will in the 'patient' to give up any
private wishes that might be found to run counter to
the will of God. Something of this kind—though not
necessarily expressed in as many terms—must be
traceable in the development of every saint's spiritual
life, and should in fact be traceable in the life of all
who are trying to serve God at all seriously. It is the
substitution of personal desires to the desires—however
little recognised at the time—of God. The soul does
not cease to *want* things, it ceases to *choose* them—for
itself. Sometimes it seems that the soul is consumed
with an even greater desire than ever it had before
it turned to God ; but what it desires *that* it offers . . .
because it wants something else still more—the will
of God.

Only those souls who can want on a generous scale
can give on a generous scale ; the anæmic followers

of Christ have very little that they can offer.[1] Thus
we so often find in the lives of the saints an apparently
ruthless disappointing of natural ambitions ; it is not
that the ambitions—human hopes, personal wishes,
special ways of doing things, plans for general improve-
ment and what not—have been *wrong*, or that, for
penance sake, the soul is being systematically blocked
along all the avenues that most attract it—such would
be to take a stern view of God's dealing with man—
rather, it is the only means whereby the soul can be
brought to that detachment whereby it can cry ' Take
all, and give me Thyself alone ! ' And this is *the*
desire, the desire of desires : the desire that God should
take . . . and that in the taking He should impart
Himself. For Cassian, that master of the spiritual
life, the sum at once of all perfection and the goal of
all contemplative prayer is ' when all love, all longing,
all desire, all seeking, all thoughts of ours, all that we
see, all that we say, all that we hope, shall be God.'
The satisfactory thing about heaven, we are told by
a considerably later exponent of the spiritual life, is
that it will be ' only Jesus.' Listen to St Teresa of
Lisieux on the subject of ' desires.' ' I would wield
the sword, I would be a priest, an apostle, a martyr,
a Doctor of the Church, I would fain accomplish the
most heroic deeds . . . the spirit of the crusader burns
within me, and I would gladly die on the battlefield
in defence of the Church ; like the prophets of old I
would be a light unto souls. I would travel the world

---

[1] But this may not be altogether their fault : they may be as
nearly bloodless as the widow in the Gospel was nearly miteless.
It is the temptation for such as these to give their gifts to God
because they are too tired to do anything else, or because they fear
the consequences of not being found sufficiently generous. ' Perfect
love casteth out fear,' and one must aim, after all, at ' perfect love.'

over to preach Thy name, O my Beloved, and raise
on heathen soil the glorious standard of the Cross . . .
I would be a missionary, but not for a few years only ;
were it possible I would wish to have been one from
the world's creation, and to remain one till the end of
time . . . open, O Jesus, the Book of Life, in which
are written the deeds of all Thy saints : each one of
those deeds I long to accomplish for Thee.'[1] And then
in the end we bring it down to one desire, one prayer,
one offering which is the peculiar prerogative of
sainthood. ' I one day sought relief in the Epistles of
St Paul,' the same saint goes on to say, ' and my
eyes lighted on the twelfth and thirteenth chapters
of the First Epistle to the Corinthians . . . the Apostle
explains how all the better gifts are nothing without
Love, and that Charity is the most excellent way of
going in safety to God. At last, I had found rest ;
I realised that love includes every vocation, that love
is all things, that love is eternal, reaching down through
the ages and stretching to the uttermost limits of the
earth. Beside myself with joy I cried out : " O Jesus,
my Love, my vocation is found at last—*my vocation
is to love.*" ' The saints are as one in this because of
Him Whom they follow—Whose ' desire ' it was to
do the will of His heavenly Father. From the saint
who wrote to the Corinthians, to the saint who wrote
to her reverend mother, there is the one overwhelming
desire—God's will. It is a hunger that is prepared
to go empty ; it is a longing that is seen in the ' restless heart ' of St Augustine and in the ' cannon-ball
heart ' of Jean Baptiste Vianney. St Catherine gives
us in a single sentence—though I am unable, I am
afraid, to find the reference—a truth which everyone

[1] *Story of a Soul*, Ch. XIII.

would admit to in theory but which has little enough meaning for most of us : ' God asketh not a perfect work but infinite desire.'

The desire is infinite in the strict sense : to be satisfied only by God. Where this desire is present it will, even though it be weak (for a thing may be infinite *and* weak—infinite in its object, weak in its subject), gradually perfect the ' works.' But this does not mean that the ' works ' will appear to the soul as ' perfect ' ; probably the whole service of such a soul will consist in seeing nothing of perfection in any of its ' works '—or even in any of its ' desires.' The service of the saint lies in the will to give and to do . . . though nothing be seen given, or found done ! If it is true that the life of a saint is heaven anticipated, it is surely a heaven without the taste of it. Holiness on earth presumably feels quite different from holiness in heaven. But ' whoso have a true desire to be at heaven, then that same time were he at heaven ghostly. For the high and the next way thither is run by *desires* and not by paces of the feet.'[1] Until, in the end, ' I have no longer any great desires, beyond that of loving till I die of love.'[2]

.   .   .   .   .

A month ago Daniel was the shy young clerical student ; now he is pitchforked into the hurly-burly of the world. And what a world ! A month ago he was drifting along in a prayerful, regular, unexciting, stay-at-home existence, and cherishing in his mind the thought of study and a lifelong service of the Law. That was his ' desire.' Now he is the exile, the

---

[1] *Cloud of Unknowing*, Ch. LX.
[2] Teresa of Lisieux, op. cit., IX.

romantic, the adventurer almost . . . and not the ghost of a notion what will become of him when he reaches Babylon. He is learning (I hope) the first steps in the lesson of sanctity. He is learning also (and this he would hardly have learned had he stayed behind in his lecture-rooms) how to deal with men, and how to be dealt with by them.

ii

If you look at a map which gives the ancient trade-routes of Asia, you will see that Daniel's caravan must have either skirted the northern end of the Dead Sea, travelling via Damascus and Palmyra and then down the Euphrates to Babylon, or else struck south to Petra and from thence across the Syrian Desert, touching Duma at about half-way. I have not the least idea as to which route was taken, and, so far as I can find out, no one else has either. The Damascus journey would have been longer from the point of view of actual mileage, but probably shorter from the point of view of time taken. Certainly it would have been more comfortable than the thirsty ride, via Petra and Duma, over seven hundred miles of desert. Either route would have meant a thoroughly detestable journey. Imagine the blistering sun, the unvarying landscape, the packed provisions,[1] the monotony of

[1] Dried fruit, salted meat, various kinds of nuts would have been the ordinary fare. This, together with the water supply, would have been carried on mule-back (camels were more expensive and, since the break with Egypt, less easily obtainable in Palestine) ; skins, baskets, crates would be slung over the backs of these unfortunate beasts and kept in position by a harness of straps or, less pleasant for the animal, a network of ropes. The skins would have been refilled whenever the caravan was lucky enough to strike an oasis, the crates would have been added to whenever the soldiers were energetic enough to trap the quail.

the time-table, the absence of any real recreation. How entirely wretched the Jewish captives must have felt as the gap widened between themselves and the land of their original ' desires.' In front of them they had nothing but the desert horizon, uncertain in its quivering film of heat. . . .

A week or so ago, when the expedition had made its dismal start in the greys and mists of the early morning, there had been a certain bitter-sweet romance about the undertaking. Now there was only the ache of separation. A week ago they had had high hopes of converting their gaolers to the Faith of Israel . . . and look at those gaolers now ! A week ago the Jews had felt that they were being led into the wilderness in much the same way that their ancestors had been led into the desert when they had come out from the land of Egypt . . . would not the Lord guide this, as He had guided the other, pilgrimage ? It seemed He would not ; the Babylonian escort were pilot enough. This time there was no pillar of fire by night nor cloud of smoke by day ; this time no manna had fallen from the heavens, no cool refreshing waters had gushed from the clefts of the relentless rocks which threw off the echo of their voices. The Jews, perhaps, had fancied—in their more hopeful moments —that the road might not be wholly innocent of adventure : that a rescue would possibly be attempted, that some nomad tribe, or even some daring party of Hebrews in pursuit, would sweep down upon the company in the night and slay the men of Babylon as they slept. Nothing of the kind, alas, had happened. Nabuchodonosor had taken no risks : the escort, on account of the valuables that accompanied the captives, was stronger and better equipped than it would ordinarily have been. No, unless most of the Chaldeans died of scurvy on the way, the Jews had not the remotest hope of escape.

· · · · ·

A herd of wild desert asses appears against the sky-line and is lost again, almost instantly, in a puff of dust. They are *free*, these beasts, with the liberty of the desert ! An eagle stops his pecking at a carcass, and, disturbed by the approach of human beings, flaps his way into the heavens until he disappears in the cloudless blue . . . he is *free*. A plump quail tumbles gently into a net . . . it has become the property of the kingdom of Babylon.

· · · · ·

Apart from desert asses,[1] quails,[2] and birds of prey, the only living things that would have been met with in the open country would have been the vermin— ubiquitous and prolific—of the sand. As Daniel and his friends looked over their shoulders in the direction

---

[1] Desert asses exist wild in Palestine to-day. Even when caught and decently treated they have never been broken in like their fellows, the domestic donkeys of the bazaars and market carts. What they live on in the desert is a mystery ; they seem to be too shy to hunt ; there is little enough to hunt in any case.

[2] Great quantities of these low-flying birds can be caught in what seems to be the most ridiculously easy way. When a flight is seen in the distance men rush out with nets (rather like those used for tennis) and stand at intervals with the nets stretched out between them. The quails are evidently too tired or too unimaginative to alter their course : they simply flop into the nets and wait for the next move in the game. This is, at any rate, the way —a way—in which the quail is trapped by Arabs to-day ; there is every reason to believe that it has always been the way of doing so. That the quail was much appreciated by the Hebrews in the desert we know from Psalm lxxvii : ' They were not defrauded of that which they craved ' ; the Jews ate, in fact, to excess on that occasion (v. 30).

of Jerusalem they would have seen a tableland of
tawny dullness, relieved occasionally by a clump
of cactus and (still more occasionally) by a sheet of
brackish water . . . a poor substitute is all this for the
City of Sion. The Hebrew children are become the
property of the kingdom of Babylon.

CHAPTER II

BABYLON

i

ESDRAS and Nehemias took three and a half months to cover the distance between Babylon and Jerusalem. I have already said that I make no guesses as to how long was spent by Daniel in traversing the same ground. Leaving aside, therefore, the question of time we can devote ourselves with greater safety—and only for the space of a single page, since it deserves no more—to the question of scene.

The proximity of the Euphrates touches up the landscape, and the proximity of fellow human beings enlivens the minds of the travellers. The journey is drawing to a close.

The valley of the great river is fertile, but the country round about is flat, arid, and uninteresting. There is a continuous stream of traffic along the west bank of the Euphrates, passing to and from Larsa, in the south, right up to Borsippar, beyond Babylon, in the north. This road must be one of the most interesting trade routes in the Near East at this particular time : on it would be seen refugees from the fallen Assyrian Empire,[1] merchants from Media in the east seizing the opportunity of a little trade before the

[1] The Tigris, on which Nineveh was situated, is only about fifty miles distant from the Euphrates in places, and it would have been safer for the dispersed Assyrians to take refuge in the south rather than among the Armenians in the north.

threatened war with Babylon, Beduin Arabs from the
west and south coming up to Babylon or Borsippar. . . .

Pleasure barges, painted and decked out with
awnings of many colours, float with a certain vulgar
majesty past the mud-hut villages which line the
Euphrates north and south of Chaldea's capital. Men
are singing in the fields ; women are washing strange
garments at the water's edge ; children are playing
in the mud ; the ancients are sleeping in the shade
of palms ; sheep are bleating as they press against
each other on the way to market ; flies swarm ; carts
sway and creak and send up clouds of gritty dust
into the faces of their passengers . . . but, for the
captives from Jerusalem, it is not such an intolerable
journey as it has been hitherto.

I am not going to attempt a reconstruction of the
way in which the convoy from Jerusalem was met at
the gates of Babylon ; we have no information about
the feeling of Chaldea towards Israel. That the captives
were technically prisoners of war is nothing very much
to go upon when we consider that there had been
virtually no war. That Nabuchodonosor had suppressed
a rebellion—or what looked as if it was going to be a
rebellion—in a distant state, a state moreover with
which Babylon had been concerned for a short time
only, may or may not have seemed important to the
man in the Babylon street. I do not know. At any
rate the man responsible for the deportation, Nabuchodonosor, does not seem to have borne his hostages
any animosity. I am ready enough (too ready, alas)
to engage in reconstruction when I have got before me
a history book, or the text itself, or one of those maps
which show a country's vegetation, rainfall, religion,
industry, and what not, but when it comes to telling

c

a story for the sake of telling a story, I feel that there are other people who could do it very much better. Also it is no part of my business to play the novelist. Let me therefore get back to Daniel and Babylon and reality.

> ' And the king appointed them [the Hebrew children] a daily provision of his own meat and of the wine of which he drank himself, that being nourished three years, afterwards they might stand before the king. Now there were among them of the children of Juda, Daniel, Ananias, Misael and Azarias. And the master of the eunuchs gave them names : to Daniel, Baltassar ; to Ananias, Sidrach ; to Misael, Misach ; and to Azarias, Abdenago.'

Directly, the above passage does not tell us a great deal ; there is much, however, that can be extracted from between the lines. Commentators will captivate your interest with citations from other parts of Scripture to show that the sending of portions from the tables of the great was no new form of compliment ; all the various offices, again, to which the title ' prince of the eunuchs ' might apply may be carefully gone into ; the precise implication attaching to the changes of name can be found to cover pages of print . . . but for our purposes it is surely better to approach the quotation from another angle altogether, and ask : what sort of a life did Daniel and his friends lead during those early years of their captivity ?

First of all, it is clear from the instructions about their diet that the Hebrew prisoners were not treated *as* prisoners, and secondly, from what we hear of the change of names, that they were not treated as free citizens. They were treated as the pets of the king's zoo were treated : thoroughly spoiled, but kept on a lead.

In the work of piecing together Daniel's early career considerable help is to be derived from the vast amount of information that has come down to us regarding the Babylon of this period. In fact one of the things that strike the casual student of the Prophet and his time is the wealth of not very important detail that is recorded of Nabuchodonosor's reign as compared with the much more important information which we would like to have, but have not got, regarding the reigns of his successors. From various different sources we know all that we could possibly want to know concerning Nabuchodonosor's garden, yet it is almost impossible to find out who succeeded him ! We hear detailed accounts of Nabuchodonosor's dealings with his slaves, yet we fail entirely to learn the names—or even the number—of his sons !

From the many books that deal with the Babylon of Daniel's and Nabuchodonosor's time I select two as being of the most general interest to the kind of reader I am envisaging ; they are *Daniel: His Life and Times* by H. Deane, and *Daniel the Prophet* by Mildred Duff and Noel Hope. The books differ widely from one another in character. The former is a serious, but not too weighty, historical study ; it is an example of the kind of work to which the best and most scholarly of Anglican divines were, towards the end of the last century, devoting their energies. The latter, Miss Duff's and Mr Hope's joint work, is, quite frankly, a very puzzling piece of writing indeed. Though as readable as the other, how this book found its way into its present form I cannot think. (It is surely a cut-down

version of a more ponderous volume ?) The authors
have collected a great deal of interesting material
from one source or another—Biblical, archælogical,
historical—but it all seems to tumble out anyhow ;
it is as if a curiosity shop had despaired of finding
buyers, and had emptied its stock of antiques into
Selfridge's Bargain Basement. The cover of the book
supports a picture of an unlikely-looking lion that is
ready to spring at you from the shelter of two rather
feathery palm trees. You think at first that the book
is intended for children (perhaps it is ?), but when you
read on (and come across ' cylinder seals ' and quotations from Herodotus, Xenophon, and the Records of
Assurbanipal) you begin to revise your judgement and
to wonder what on earth is the public to which Miss
Duff and Mr Hope are making their appeal. You
become possessed of the uneasy feeling that you are
having your leg pulled. And on top of all this you can
buy the book for a shilling ! But, as I say, it is well
worth reading.

ii

If opportunities were given to Daniel for exploring
the city, and if his restrictions were mostly of a kind
that affected his spiritual rather than his temporal
comfort, then Babylon might be considered—from the
human point of view—no mean prison in which to
suffer exile.[1] Daniel might have fared a great deal
worse. In matters artistic and literary Babylon was
well in advance of Damascus and Jerusalem at this

[1] We shall examine the nature of the spiritual restrictions when
we come to them in the text ; it is worth while noticing here, however, that the changes of name involved, in the case of each of the
four Hebrews, a substitution of Babylonian gods for the God of
Israel.

time, and its fame as an industrial centre was pro-
verbial. Jeremias refers to Babylon (foretelling its
destruction) as ' the hammer of the whole earth,' and
certainly it was a hammer that was never still ; the
noise of its hammering had drowned whatever echo
there had been from the ' loudest ' civilised city of
the previous generation, Nineveh. Daniel had of course
never seen Nineveh, but he had known Jerusalem well
enough, and if (as I am secretly inclined to think) he
had passed through Damascus on his journey from the
Jordan to the Euphrates, then he can have been left
in no doubt as to which of the great centres he had
visited was the most ' go-ahead.'

A number of vast undertakings were in progress at
the time which we are considering, and Daniel—unless
he was a very abnormal young man—would have
watched them with a lively interest. Nabuchodonosor
was more a builder than he was, even, a general.
His plans for the ' new Babylon ' must have appeared
too wildly extravagant for words to the citizens of the
ancient town.[1] In an incredibly short space of time a
completely new Babylon seems to have grown up ; to
walk around the city walls you had to make a journey
of forty miles ! These walls, incidentally, were seventy
feet high, and so thick that you could have driven two

[1] In spite of the rough treatment Babylon had received at the
hands of the Assyrians during the previous century there was
probably a great deal of the old city left. We know, for instance,
that there were remains of the tower of Babel (from which the city
took its name), because an inscription states that Nabuchodonosor
repaired it. The origins of Babylon, therefore, are prehistoric ; it
is one of the oldest cities of the world ; Babylonia is ' a kingdom
which claims a succession of kings for over four hundred years
before the Deluge, and nearly forty thousand years since that
event ' (Deane, *Daniel*). All that Nabuchodonosor was doing was
to put new blood into old veins—veins which had been so blue for
generations that they had ceased to be of any practical use.

chariots abreast along the entire circumference of Babylon. The Duff and Hope book already cited says that there were *three* walls round the city and that the middle one was ninety feet high, but I believe this is no longer considered likely. It is worth noting that the bricks with which the new Babylon was built— whether used in walls, palaces, temples or monuments —each bear the stamp of the king's name. Nabuchodonosor was, as we shall see, a great artist, so he may be allowed, I suppose, to sign his pictures.

Either at the time of Daniel's arrival in Babylon or a little later a bridge was being built over the Euphrates. This work is said to have been executed in stone and not in the baked brick which was then so popular. Another tremendous enterprise was the restoration of the temple of Bel. Nabuchodonosor was nothing if not generous towards the many deities of his capital ; this is rather to be wondered at because he himself worshipped at one shrine only—that of the god Merodach, or Marduk. According to T. G. Pinches —in his remarkable book, *The Old Testament in the Light of the Historical Records of Assyria and Babylonia*— Nabuchodonosor was as ready to establish shrines for his subjects (I put it thus, rather than say he erected shrines to Babylonian gods ; he was far more eager, at first at any rate, to placate his subjects than their gods) *outside* Babylon as he was to renovate the temples that lay within his walls.

If Daniel looked on with approval at the building of bridges and gates and towers he can hardly have been pleased at the industry that was being expended upon the restoration of false worship. If, in addition, Hebrew labour was being requisitioned for this purpose Daniel would have been rendered very miserable indeed. He himself, by reason of his rank and royal favour, would have had little cause to fear enlistment in the fatigue parties, but he would have resented the insult to the blood of Juda. But as a matter of fact it hardly seems likely that many Jewish slaves were ' sweated ' in Babylon at this time ; for the very simple reason that there were not enough to ' sweat.'[1]

With fewer misgivings Daniel would have watched the construction of Nabuchodonosor's famous ' hanging gardens.' These (' as every schoolboy knows ') number among the Wonders of the World. Nabuchodonosor planned these gardens in order to cure the homesickness of one of his wives. The lady in question was of Medish origin, and it evidently troubled her to gaze out over the landscape surrounding Babylon which was relieved only by dull hummocky sand-hills ; so Nabuchodonosor changed the landscape for her. In the pages that follow I hope it will be made clear what a great soul—apart from what a great personality—Nabuchodonosor possessed ; I have therefore no scruple in saying here that we do not see him at his best in the early years of his reign : this hanging-garden side to his character is more an evidence of the super-man's weakness than of the super-man's strength. The great monarch was showing the world that he could use material creation—however expensive—to serve his own ends. Admittedly he showed himself skilful in the control of the material commandeered, but one ventures to think that he had never really thought out the principle of the thing. God had chosen to place

---

[1] I should add that Deane seems to take it for granted that large numbers of Jews were taken away from Jerusalem and brought to Babylon with Daniel and his companions. We must remember that there were at least four *other* stages in the Captivity. The first convoy, Daniel's, I take to have been a comparatively small one.

Babylon in the middle of a plain, and here was
Nabuchodonosor deciding that it might be more convenient on the whole to have it in the Rockies. The
' hanging gardens ' were not *true* to Chaldea.

One wonders what Daniel thought of the ' hanging
gardens.' He would have watched the process of bringing soil from the canal which was then being made
between the Euphrates and the Tigris. He would have
seen the great boulders being dragged from distant
quarries. Terrace upon terrace—all excavated soil—
would mount up almost, it would have seemed, while
he waited. Then he would have seen, when once the
ground had been prepared, the system on which the
gardens were to be irrigated ; he would have marvelled
at the daring which brought evergreens (in that
climate !) to decorate the grassy slopes ; he would have
watched the arrival, in cages, of whatever birds and
beasts were chosen by Nabuchodonosor to roam the
garden enclosure ; he would, with his Hebrew sense of
thrift, have estimated the cost of all this. Yes, the
thing was fabulously extravagant ; it was quite out
of the region of a botanical experiment, it was altering
the geography of the land. One hopes that other
instincts besides that of economy were roused within
the Prophet ; one hopes that he would have seen in
this act of Nabuchodonosor a certain very offensive
vulgarity : a millionaire king was doing with the hill
country of Media what many a millionaire American
has done since with an English country house ; and
there is something about this juggling with things that
are meant to be left where they are that offends against
the right ordering of things. A deeper instinct would
have been stirred by the thought of what all this was
doing to the men actually engaged on the work, and

what the poor would have to suffer in the way of subsequent taxation : blood and sweat were included (so
Daniel would have thought) in the irrigation scheme
of Nabuchodonosor's 'hanging garden.' May we go
one step further, and put it into the mind of Daniel to
foresee that it would be just this sort of thing which
would prove the undoing of Babylon's king ? Love of
display, disregard of people's feelings (apart from the
homesick feelings of his wife),[1] and a regrettable
muddle-headedness about the balance of values were
to bring shame upon the house of Nabuchodonosor.
How much, one wonders, did Daniel see of this ?

iii

If Daniel derived a certain melancholy interest from
all that was going on in Babylon, it was an interest
that can have had little to do with his spiritual life.
The home of the Prophet's soul—as of his body—was
Jerusalem, and even allowing that he was prepared to
make the best of it as far as his being exiled was concerned it must have been exceedingly difficult for his
interior course to adjust itself to the new conditions.
Religiously Daniel had next to nothing in common
with those among whom he was now compelled to
dwell ; he could sing with the Psalmist : ' By the waters
of Babylon we sat and wept, when we remembered
Sion . . . how shall we sing the song of the Lord in
a strange land ? If I forget thee, O Jerusalem, let my
right hand be forgotten.'[2] The ' song of the Lord '
was not heard in Babylon ; Daniel was cut off from the

[1] For the oppression and injustice which Nabuchodonosor exercised at the beginning of his reign, see Pusey, *Lectures on Daniel
the Prophet*, p. 559.

[2] Psalm cxxxvi, 1–5.

daily liturgical worship of the Chosen People. Everywhere he would have had to come in contact with the
false philosophy, the false culture, the false spirituality
of Chaldea. Therein, surely, lay the sting of Daniel's
exile. ' The Catholic who, by circumstances, is obliged
to quit his own land,' writes Fr Leen in his book, *The
Likeness of Christ*, ' finds one great comfort in the
isolation he suffers when living among those who differ
from him in language and mentality. In the familiar
rites and practices of his religion he establishes contact
with those around him and annihilates the distance
that separates him from what had been the ordinary
setting of his existence. In the presence of the Blessed
Sacrament he establishes contact with home and
kindred. There the feeling of loneliness and isolation
is much mitigated if not quite dispelled.' Daniel must
have craved for some such companionship as this. No
outward ordinances, no regular sacrifices as appointed
by the Law, no religious festivals, no centre of worship
—it must all have been very galling indeed. And then,
over and above the ache of loss, for him to see the
immense care that was being taken all around him to
please a god, or gods, whom he knew to be as useless
as the peacocks that strutted in Babylon's hanging
gardens . . . more useless in fact, because at least
the peacocks were pleasant creatures to watch.

iv

And so we picture the young man Daniel threading
his way through the noisy streets of Babylon ; he is
making for a favourite spot of his on the western
wall . . .

As he hurries along, eager to get in as much time

as possible at his meditations, he sees a hundred sights
that will prove as many sources of distraction. He
sees the merchants sitting among their gorgeous fabrics
and saying things which he does not particularly want
to hear. He sees cart-loads of food being taken to
the Temples of Bel and Merodach. He sees dancing-
girls, all beads and bracelets, staring at him from
not-very-virtuous-looking doorways. He sees gangs
of exhausted slaves—Assyrians, Medes, Egyptians,
Armenians. He sees—and his soul sickens at this
sight more than at any other—a number of his own
countrymen conforming to the manners of the people
of the land. Daniel's soul is filled with a loathing
for Babylon : it is doing for Juda what the not-very-
virtuous-looking doorways have failed to do for him.

Arrived at his look-out on the top of the wall Daniel
would gaze across the plain (the gardens were on the
other, the eastern, side of the city) and wonder if it
would ever be his lot to set out in that direction again.
We think of him taking the prayer of Jonas and making
it his own : ' I am cast out of the sight of Thy eyes,
but yet I shall see Thy holy Temple again . . . and
Thou shalt bring up my life from corruption, O Lord
my God.'[1] Both prophets had the same lesson to
learn : that it is a waste of energy to dream of a temple
made with hands. Of our own lives we must make
our ' temple,' and dwell therein in confidence with
God. Souls may pray, using Jonas's prayer, for a
return to the appointed temple of God, but they must
not tell God how the prayer is to be answered. Nor
may they plan dramatic returns on their own account.
Daniel, gazing in the direction of Jerusalem, is not
building castles in the air ; he is, if he is praying rightly,

[1] Jonas ii, 5–7.

building a temple in his own soul—and inviting the Lord to come and dwell in it. Let us hope that if his prayer at the beginning was along the lines of Jacob's ' terrible is this place,' it was, by the time that he began to make a move in the direction of the city below, a continuation of that same patriarch's reflection : ' indeed the Lord is in this place and I knew it not.'[1] Is it too fanciful to think of Daniel going one step further and saying in his prayer to God— still with the words of the exile Jacob—' this is no other but the house of God and the gate of heaven ? ' Yes, Babylon must become for Daniel the ' house of God ' ; not the kind of house which he, Daniel, would have chosen, but evidently the one selected from all eternity by the Lord. Yes, this western gate over which he was standing must become for him ' the gate of heaven ' : no longer to be thought of as preventing his going out . . . rather, as making possible his spiritual coming in. The gate of Babylon was from now onwards to be looked upon as opening to the home of the Beloved.

v

Daniel comes down from his corner on the top of the western wall, and makes towards the place of his detention. The sun has set by now, and the lamps are being lit in the booths. In the half-light it is more easy to escape the notice which was excited by his previous walk through the city. On his side, however, it is not altogether easy to escape the sights and sounds which that very wicked city is able to provide. Perhaps (reflects Daniel) Babylon is not quite such a cosmo-

[1] Genesis xxviii, 16, 17.

politan centre as those that lie on one of the principal
trade routes of the Near East, and perhaps it has not
all the moral disadvantages of being a port, but
certain it is that the resident population is mixed
enough.[1] The bazaar is a patchwork, constantly
changing, of vivid colours and sharp shadows. The
dancing flames of pitch-torches give to the restless
scene a touch of transitory energy which, to the sober
young Hebrew Prophet, is symbolical of the Babylon
in which his lot is cast—blaring, ephemeral, hot.
He smells the brewing of strange liquors, the burning
of heady incense-sticks, the cooking of spiced meats,
and the sickly but seductive perfumes which, from the
clothes and hair of the passers-by that throng him in
the crowd, make their unanswered bid for the capitula-
tion of his ideal.

Daniel draws near to the more respectable quarter
of the town, the part which is occupied by the nobles
and the city magnates. Here everything is quieter
and cleaner and, to the outward eye, more in order.
He hears perhaps the melancholy note of the hautboy
(the scion of some ancient house is engaged in his
evening music-practice), and sees the splendid sight
of a general or a minister of the crown going out to
dine. The walls of the wealthy line the road, and

[1] Chaldean conquests and Chaldean wealth had done for its
capital what culture was to do for Athens, what diplomacy was to
do for Rome, and what climate and fashion was to do for Antioch.
Babylon was in some ways the Hollywood (rather than the Paris) of
the Near East ; only it was a Hollywood with a difference, and the
difference amounted to a very real—though very misguided—sense
of the supernatural. Babylon could boast of most of the tricks and
toys of contemporary civilisation ; it would have been more than
a match, as we have seen, for the cities of Egypt and Assyria in
matters of learning and sport ; but over and above its merits as a
scientific, academic, and fun-city the Chaldean capital most
assuredly ranked as a centre of worship as well.

he catches glimpses of paved courtyards and vine-grown trellises. He hears the cool plashing of water from some fountain whose marble basins have probably come to Babylon from workshops further, even, than from where he himself has come. A horse (perhaps as homesick as himself) neighs with unspeakable feeling from a distant stable. And Daniel knocks upon the door of a porter's lodge. . . .

' This is no other than the house of God and the gate of heaven.' Has the Prophet grasped, I wonder, as he follows a uniformed figure across the moonlit space which separates the gate-house from the palace steps, that his prison is not a prison but a cloister ? And that the man in front of him with the keys is really an angel in disguise ?

' The Lord is in this place and I knew it not.' It is ' terrible ' no longer.

A heavy door swings to, and the ' angel ' goes back to his supper. That is the end of Daniel's monthly *exeat*.

CHAPTER III

DANIEL'S DECLARATION OF POLICY
(Daniel i.)

i

' Daniel purposed in his heart that he would not
be defiled with the king's table, nor with the wine
which he drank ; and he requested the master of
the eunuchs that he might not be defiled.'

WE owe much to the careful, inquisitive, relentless
spade of the archæologist ; we know, for
instance, where Daniel was lodged at the time of his
making the above decision and request.

Excavations show how Nabuchodonosor pulled down
the royal dwelling which had been good enough for
his father, Nabopolassar, and erected a new and
enlarged palace on the old site. So enlarged, in fact,
was the new building that it spread over the Euphrates,
ending up in a sort of gigantic annexe, which was
as big, if not bigger, than the kingly residence itself.
Communication between what was really two palaces
was maintained by a traffic bridge over the water ;
and, doubtless, Nabuchodonosor derived the keenest
satisfaction and enjoyment from running the whole
establishment as if it had been a four-roomed villa.
The temple of Marduk was on the same side—that is,
the east side—of the river as were the ' official ' or
' guest ' quarters, and was at the same time within

easy view of the king's private balconies. Thus was
enclosed by what might be called the ' palace precincts '
an area of some 150 to 200 acres.[1] Besides this—the
principal group of buildings in the city—there were,
at intervals along the four walls, lesser citadels
which sat at watch over the more important gates
of Babylon.[2]

It is almost certain that Daniel and his Hebrew
friends, Ananias, Misael, and Azarias, were housed in
the eastern building on the king's domain ; this was
the part of the establishment which was intended to
provide both for the overflow of Nabuchodonosor's
vast retinue and for such visiting sovereigns or dele-
gates who happened to be staying in the capital.
Under the same hospitable roof would be included a
sort of internment camp ; the palace could offer every
comfort to those within its walls, and it could at the
same time prevent its occupants from taking undue
interest in the things that were going on abroad.
There were dungeons as well as drawing-rooms in the
residence over the water ; enjoyment of royal hospitality was a precarious privilege in the days of
Nabuchodonosor, king of Babylon.

[1] See St Clair, *Buried Cities and Bible Countries*, p. 365.
[2] Of these gates the one which has lent itself the most readily
to reconstruction is the Ishtar Gate. Built by Nabuchodonosor on
Babylon's ' Processional Way,' this gate must have been as much
an ornament as it was a defence. Designs of animals were enamelled
on the inner face of the building. Most of Nabuchodonosor's
decoration was carried out in low relief, which, against a ground of
unglazed brick, must have looked very effective indeed. The brick-
work of Babylon's principal citadel was so carefully laid that
excavated blocks of it are preserved intact to this day. Burnt
bricks were used for surface work only, sun-dried bricks being the
commoner material for construction purposes. I believe the remains
of kilns are still to be found in the district surrounding Babylon's
ruins. (I think I have read this somewhere, but I am unable to
verify it ; perhaps I am thinking of the brick-kilns that are still in
use not far from Nineveh.)

But apart from the floating population that drifted through (or ultimately sank in) the Palace of Guests, there seems to have existed some sort of resident community. The common life—such as it was—would appear to have been academic rather than religious : a brotherhood of ' wise men ' who wrestled with their wisdom and imparted their conclusions to students of promise. Research . . . experiments . . . lectures ; and every now and then a sort of ' summer school,' to the sessions of which the king, and those of his court who were of a scholarly bent, were invited ; learning was patronised here in the seventh century B.C., and learning lent her patronage in return.

Daniel then, with his three companions, had for fellow-lodgers a mixed band of astrologers, magicians, philosophers, and theologians. The entire household was, as we shall see from more than one event recorded in the narrative, immediately responsible to the king : like everything else in the land of Chaldea, the royal ' guests ' were at the disposal of one whose demands could be as unexpected as they were sometimes exacting. But this is to anticipate.

We have seen that Daniel—to use his own words— was instructed in the ' learning and the tongue of the Chaldeans ' ; to have to submit to the teaching of unbelievers, even though theology were not included in the curriculum, would have been no small mortification to one who had learned in the schools of Jerusalem. We have also seen that Daniel was ' appointed a daily provision of the king's meat ' ; Nabuchodonosor, not satisfied with providing for the minds of his charges, took good care to provide for their bodies also : he saw in person to their *cuisine*. With what result ? ' Daniel purposed in his heart that he would not be

D

defiled with the king's table.' Having made up his
mind on the *principle* at issue, the Prophet embarked
upon a very practical course in securing that principle's
recognition. He did not push his plate away and go
hungry ; nor did he strike the attitude of martyrdom
and bid for the pity of his gaolers ; neither were
forbidden meats flung—with religious fervour and
unerring aim—at unbelieving heads. . . . What happened
was that Daniel simply asked if special arrangements
might not be made to satisfy his conscience. ' He
requested the master of the eunuchs that he might
not be defiled.' What a curious interview there must
have been between the two ! And from Daniel's
point of view it was, in part at any rate, a success ;
the text goes on : ' God gave to Daniel grace and mercy
in the sight of the prince of the eunuchs.' But that
is as far as it went, because the heart of the prince of
the eunuchs failed him at the last moment and the
petition was refused ; Daniel was told ' I fear the
king who hath appointed you meat and drink, who
if he should see your faces leaner than those of the
other youths, you shall endanger my head to the
king.' The prince of the eunuchs evidently knew
his Nabuchodonosor.

Daniel saw the force of the prince's argument, and
he also summed up the man who had advanced it ; a
new approach would have to be found. It was. ' And
Daniel said to Malasar, whom the prince of the eunuchs
had appointed over Daniel, Ananias, Misael, and
Azarias : Try, I beseech thee, thy servants for ten
days, and let pulse be given us to eat and water to
drink, and look upon our faces and the faces of the
children that eat of the king's meat ; and as thou shalt
see, deal with thy servants.' Daniel has studied

human nature : he knows that where a man cannot be tempted by a straightforward appeal to do something he does not want to do, he can often be won round by a challenge or a bet. The prince of the eunuchs being presumably of too exalted a dignity, Malasar, his second in command, is chosen by Daniel to be the recipient of the terms of his speculation. Daniel knows that Malasar stands less risk of incurring the anger of the king : excuse can always be made that instructions which have been handed down through a chain of officials must always be liable to a margin of error—especially if they relate to something so variable as a menu. Malasar decides to take the risk.

' And when he had heard these words he tried them for ten days.' A temporary trial, without prejudice, was to be given to whatever *régime* Daniel should draw up. If, after that, wasted frames, haggard looks, peevish tempers, and sleepless nights were to proclaim the disregarding of the king's edict then Daniel and his friends would have to grapple as before with the many courses and the many cups—and thank the good god Bel for what they got.

' And after ten days their faces appeared fairer and fatter than all the children that did eat of the king's meat. So Malasar took their portions and the wine that they should drink, and he gave them pulse. And to these children God gave knowledge and understanding of every book and wisdom, but to Daniel the understanding also of visions and dreams.'

Far, then, from showing the slightest decline, the faces of the four young men proclaimed the sagacity of the proposal ; the arrangement was adopted permanently.

Now this incident—as all those who have meditated or commented upon the passage have realised—is an illustration of what confidence in God can effect. It is also an instance of the success which attends man's effort to abide by the completest possible observance of God's laws. But apart from these considerations we have, I think, a further lesson to learn from Daniel's action : a lesson which is part spiritual, part practical —the lesson of (as the saying is) ' how to go about it.' Let us take the facts.

Daniel is making a very spirited bid for as much of the law as is compatible with the circumstance in which he is placed. He is among unbelievers—that he cannot help ; he is made to change his name to Baltassar—that too he cannot help ; but when it comes to his eating forbidden foods and keeping pagan feasts he resists to the uttermost. He has reason to believe, moreover, that the Lord is with him in his obstinacy : God supported his fasts and ' added to him in his knowledge.' The application of all this is fairly obvious, but as a matter of fact there is more in the business (I think) than meets the eye ; as regards ourselves, let us see how far it helps us to cope with a concrete case. I do not mean necessarily the concrete case of mortification in food (because after all the regulation of appetite is not man's chief concern, ' meat doth not commend us to God ; for neither if we eat shall we have the more, nor if we eat not shall we have the less '[1]), but rather the whole question as to what steps should be taken towards satisfying the need for (or the desire for—which is the same thing) penance.

[1] 1 Corinthians viii, 8.

Briefly to go over the points of the story again : Daniel first of all asked the master of the eunuchs if he could practise a mortification which he believed that his conscience was urging him to undertake. The answer he received was a negative one, but it was not such an answer as to forbid further consideration of the subject ; it merely stated that the particular authority questioned regretted its inability to comply with the request. Thus on the first count there is no decision either way. If anything, the results would seem to show that Daniel's conscience is at fault somewhere. In the absence of a definite ruling Daniel asks again, but asks a lesser authority this time, and suggests a test which should both show to his superior whether or not the proposal was feasible, and at the same time prove to his own, Daniel's, satisfaction whether or not the inspiration came from God. We know the result : authority was satisfied, the resolution was justified. Daniel, knowing that every obstacle was now removed, could go ahead with an easy conscience. He did.

A soul feels a call to penance. Is he to follow that call ? Obviously he must obtain official sanction. He asks and is refused. But *how* is he refused ? This makes all the difference, because provided he has not been told to keep silence, he may—and perhaps should—ask again. He must always remember that the calls of grace are probably *meant* to meet with opposition at first. Well, he asks a second time, or a third, or a fourth, and is finally given leave for a trial ; the effects of this trial may then be taken as tolerably adequate indication, if not actual proof, of the genuineness of the call. *But always and at every step there is the indifference born of faith which leaves room for the signified will of*

God. And the signified will of God may very well
lie in quite a different direction from that in which
it was expected to be found. Detachment, utter
abandonment, the glad yielding to whatever mould
may be pressed down upon us by God's hand—these
are proof enough against deception. When every
faculty is at rest in its proper object—God—and when
every longing is united in one single, unemotional, willed
desire—to do His will—then a great calm comes down
upon the soul, and the soul has the leisure to listen, and
the leisure to decide. Thus again do we find ourselves
back at our ' desires ' ; or rather back at our one desire
—to do the will of Him Who sent us. Given that, it
will matter little whether our wishes to do great
penance are realised or no.

ii

Arising out of (rather than ' in opposition to ') the
above, a number of mildly querulous voices make themselves heard.

' Was it not rather *singular* on Daniel's part ' (says
one of them) ' to make a parade of his religious
practice ? Isn't it supposed to be more humble to
accept the existing situation and sink one's preferences ?
What about this *beaten track* we are always being told
about ? '

' Why, having once submitted to a course of Chaldean
instruction ' (is the objection of another), ' did Daniel
refuse to be nourished with Chaldean foods ? Don't
you think he probably studied because he was fond of
study, and fasted because he was full of fads ? Or
isn't it even possible that he wanted to show Babylon
what real asceticism was like—knowing that Babylon

would not be particularly impressed if he merely cut his lectures ? '

' Isn't there any test ' (asks a third voice—longing to get the thing straight once and for all), ' which lets us see the difference between the penances to be undertaken and the penances to be suspected ? '

These and a crop of similar difficulties are of a kind that are constantly being put to priests in the confessional, to retreat-givers, to novice-masters, and to directors in general, so the whole matter of voluntary mortification is presumably of sufficiently practical interest to justify investigation here.

Let us take the first question : How much of our religious life is to be allowed to *show* ? To begin with —and approaching the thing from very far away—I suppose we would agree that there are few who have the courage to defy the world in which they live. Let alone the question as to whether it is right or wrong to do so, there are few (I say) who have the *courage*. The easiest thing is always to accept the standards of our fellows—even when we know those standards to be so false that they will probably involve trouble later on. We know this ; very good. The second step is concerned not so much with what we know as with what we must remember. We must remember, surely, that one of a ' peculiar people ' must be prepared to be—if necessary—peculiar. Fr Martindale, in his book, *The Waters of Twilight*, puts this very pertinent remark on the lips of one of his characters: ' Obviously, what we're out after is life. Christ came that we might have it more abundantly . . . well, somehow any very vital person seems to act a little cross-ways. He doesn't just hurry up the going concern. He pulls it a little askew. Even when he doesn't mean to. And after

all, who are the interesting folk ? Who really stimulate
one and buck one up ? People who go off at a tack—
oh, not rebelliously their own, but still, what the toe-
the-line school would call crooked.' Yes, Fr Martindale
is right : the saint is *bound* to pull things a little
askew, *even when he doesn't mean to*. In fact, he most
certainly mustn't mean to—for the *sake* of pulling
them askew. The saint, don't you see, views things
in a different perspective, and in his clearer, truer,
vision he sees that the position of some of those things
has—if the order to be arrived at is the order ordained
by God—to be altered. He has got to juggle with the
' existing order of things.' He doesn't *like* juggling ;
he doesn't *want* to juggle ; he hates the irritation
and publicity which his juggling may possibly bring
about. But he juggles all the same. And, as a matter
of fact, the outward effects of the saint's defiance of
this or that convention—unpleasant as those outward
effects are (the pain given to others, the attention
attracted to self, the misunderstandings, the ridicule
and so on)—will probably not cost him anything like
as much discomfort as having to provide an answer
to the conflicting calls that are whispering in his own
soul. How is he going to answer this—which is so
very nearly valid : ' The most perfect thing is to do
what everyone else does ' ? And this : ' The Cross
must not be sought out if it makes you conspicuous as
a cross-bearer ' ? Or this : ' Common consent is the
surest seal to the Will of God ' ? These secret whisper-
ings within the soul, all of them urging surrender on
the best possible motives, are the more upsetting when
they are backed by arguments that relate to the
particular person concerned and not necessarily to
anyone else. ' You have failed before in just these

circumstances,'—is one such argument—' you will never persevere on . . . and on . . . and on . . .' Or again : ' It's perhaps unfortunate, but with your rather unusual temperament you *need* more outlet than other people.' Which in practice becomes : ' Don't *overdo* it : your health *and* the kind of work you're doing demand plenty of sleep and bigger meals.'[1] And then there is that last whisper—the most insidious of all because sounded under cover of humility— ' Penance may be meant for the saints, but you're far from being a saint and it would be presumption on your part to undertake anything beyond the bare duties of your state ; penance isn't meant for people like you.' (But *isn't* it ? Is not penance meant to show that love is there ? Take the ordinary sufferings that come—yes, by all means—but express your readiness to do so by showing a free familiarity with pain.)

It comes to this then : that we are not to try to be singular ; that we are to try, further, *not* to be singular ; but that most of all we are to try and forget all about singularity. If the attention of others is fixed upon ourselves, and if at the same time we would far rather it were not so fixed, it is not likely that our humility will suffer as a result. However we look at it we are always driven back to the truth that no two souls are made alike, and that therefore each must go to God in its own way. Everyone is made ' in the image and likeness of God ' and not in the image and likeness of anyone else—still less in the image and likeness of a

---

[1] I am not suggesting for a moment that health and work should be disregarded when it comes to selecting practices of mortification. Obviously to do so would be wrong. I am only saying that for those of us who enjoy rude health it is perhaps not always necessary to take advantage of the dispensations—say with regard to fasting in Lent—that are permitted by the Church.

whole *lot* of people. Now because God is not like anyone else there is no reason why anyone should be like
any *one* else—still less like *everyone* else. If God wants
the way of some souls to appear outwardly as a
'singular' way, the best thing those souls can do is to
forget about the 'singularity' and concentrate upon
the 'way.' While it would be as well for those who
are tempted to criticise such individuality to bear in
mind that the God-centred people of this world are
bound to be—for that very reason—ex-centric.

I hope it will be understood that I am not advocating
singularity. Or even, strictly speaking, defending it.
I am merely accounting for it.

．　　　．　　　．　　　．　　　．

Not only Daniel's easy-going guardians, but his
fellow-captives also—at least the foreign ones, the
Egyptians, Assyrians, and Medes—must have very
soon realised that what the Israelites were after was
something quite different from what they themselves
had conceived of as being due to religion. The pleasures
of the worldly city to which the exiles had access
evidently meant nothing to Daniel and his three
friends. The way of life chosen by these Hebrews
('insisted upon' one might almost say) was retired,
simple, and austere ; a large place in their horarium
was given to prayer ; the observance of Jewish 'days'
was, as far as was possible under the circumstances,
kept. In fact the 'Hebrew children' were altogether
'singular.'

．　　　．　　　．　　　．　　　．

There is now the second difficulty to be met : why
it was that Daniel consented to sit at the feet of pagan

pedagogues and yet refused to sit before pagan dishes.

The Prophet (as we know from the way in which he accepted the dinner of Habacuc)[1] could enjoy a meal as much as anybody. So it was not because he was fastidious or, strictly speaking, because he was afraid of being greedy that he fasted. The meats of the king's table had no more power to draw his soul from God than had the doctrines of the king's school. Quite simply, Daniel decided to take a strong line in the matter of food because he knew very well that if he did not take a strong line *somewhere* he would find it uncommonly difficult to keep to even the minimum of his religious observance. And, in point of fact, the food question was probably the only one on which he stood the remotest chance of getting his own way. Daniel would have had little scruple with regard to his studies ; the vain philosophies of Babylon meant no more to him than the legendary sagas meant to his fellow-prisoners—rather less. Also, as I have suggested, they would have been very difficult to avoid. Daniel, then, rebelled against forbidden meats for a number of reasons—chief among which was the thought of what he was laying himself open to were he to take the line of least resistance. And he had not only himself to consider ; there were the other Hebrew students whose spokesman he was and for whom he was, in part at least, responsible. The case for all of them was the same : attendance at lectures began and ended there ; acceptance of prohibited foods was the thin end of the wedge. Before long Daniel—were he to make any concessions at all—would find himself answering invitations of every kind. Chaldean

[1] xiv, 37.

matrons would have been only too pleased to secure the
presence of this eligible young man (and party) at
whatever entertainments the Babylon season should
happen to provide. Had he so wished, Daniel could
have become a familiar figure in the *salons*, at the
circus, on the field, and among the guests who were
privileged to attend the much-coveted (but probably
not at all festive) hanging-garden-parties. And it
might go further : who knew but what the priests of
some local god or goddess might not require the
attendance of the Hebrews to swell the numbers of a
procession or a pagan revel ? Daniel had not only the
luxuries of the Babylonian court to fight against, he
had the possibility of giving scandal in matters affecting
worship to consider. Daniel was not ' of this world,'
but he knew enough of this world to see that a com-
promise with it would be fatal : all the more were
dispensations in food and drink to be avoided because
a generous Chaldean licence here would stand for the
' world ' in which a generous study of Chaldean letters
most certainly would not. And it was to the ' world '
that the Prophet refused to surrender—even in such
a little matter as that of food.

.   .   .   .   .

To-day, in one of the great halls of the palace, there
is to be a display of learning, a tournament of wits.
It is now three years[1] since Daniel began his course
of Chaldean studies. Professors and students from
remote parts of the Empire are present and every
branch of intellectual pursuit is represented. Nabuchodonosor, glorious in his cloak of gold, is led to his
place under the royal canopy. There is a certain

[1] i, 5 ; cf. 18.

restrained excitement : worshippers at the shrine of brain are naturally less demonstrative than those who burn incense before the gods of brawn ; the enthusiasm displayed at this assembly is nothing if not well bred.

An aged scholar mounts a festooned platform and introduces his pupil to Babylon's intelligentsia. A shy son of Chaldea, weighed down with much learning, whines his exordium ; the performance has begun.

Address follows address ; the same polished periods, the same university accent, the same gestures . . . and the same expression on the faces of the audience. The king, himself no mean scholar, is seen to fidget ; he drums with his finger-tips on the arm of his chair ; he twists his list of competitors into strange shapes ; his mind is elsewhere ; he is not amused. Towards the end of the time allotted Daniel takes his turn on the rostrum. The Hebrew's learning, immeasurably superior to anything that has been exhibited hitherto, is appreciated at its true worth : Daniel has ' arrived.' Daniel's three friends are waved, one by one, up those steps that have seen the making and the marring of careers. Like the Prophet, they too acquit themselves very creditably ; so much so that our author is able to say (blushing modestly as he bends over the page) that ' there was not found among them all '—all the university students, that is of which the native scholars should obviously have come out top—' such as Daniel, Ananias, Misael, and Azarias.' An additional hint as to the success of the performance is to be found in the wording of the verse which follows : ' *ten times* better than all the diviners and wise men that were in his kingdom [did the king prove the sons of Israel to be].' From this it is not difficult to estimate the form in which Nabuchodonosor expressed his approval: ' There now,' we can hear him say to his ministers and professors, ' what did I tell you about these little Hebrew friends of mine ? The specimens which you have selected to throw glory upon the educational systems of Babylon are unable to hold a candle to the students who have been grounded in Jerusalem. At least ten times as promising (I should say at a venture) were the Jewish competitors . . . see if you can't get our young people up to that standard.' And Nabuchodonosor sweeps past the file of bowing savants, and out by the great door into the sun.

As the Chaldean prodigies repair to their con- gratulatory banquet (without, in the opinion of some, having fully earned it) the Hebrew youths betake themselves to their frugal fare of herbs and pulse. Study is in one pigeon-hole, eating is in another ; but both are attended by the same zeal, the zeal for the Lord the God of hosts.

.   .   .   .   .

There is still the third and last difficulty to be dealt with : Why can't we have a definite ruling about which are the penances to practise and which aren't ; which are the saints to follow and which aren't ; what is singular and what isn't ; what is submission to the will of God and what is just laziness ?

If we can settle the above we have settled the whole thing.

For purposes of illustration let us take the expert, the man who is judged to have answered these and other problems—I mean the saint.

History would seem to show that the saint can, when

he comes up against questions of practical conduct such as we have been considering, judge the exact lengths to which he may go in answering what he believes to be God's calls. He is apparently able to test his impulses in such a way that what seem to us, perhaps, outrages against established convention are, in actual fact, so many stepping-stones in his approach to God. Does this mean that the saint has an extra sense which is not granted to you and me ? The saint (it would seem) is subject to exactly the same kind of ' whisper ' that is found to bother us (we have listened to the line adopted by these whispers—health, humility, work and so on) and yet he is able to answer immovably and without subsequent misgivings : ' God wants of me *this* . . .' And he goes ahead and does it. Now how does he *know* that this is right ?

First of all let us console ourselves with this consideration : far from having more than we have (in the way of possessing an additional judging faculty) the saint has, if anything, less. But what he *has* got, he uses to the full. That is to say he takes very good care not to have any standards to judge by that are not dictated by the here-and-now will of God. We, on the other hand, allow *all kinds of influences*— some of them extremely worthy—to play a part. Even granted that we are intent (as are the saints) upon doing the will of God in any one decision to be made or line of conduct to be followed there are a number of artificial supports with which we—so to speak—buttress ourselves ; while for the saint, going about it in a different way, these same influences are left on one side (not, perhaps, consciously or deliberately, but simply because they are off the *direct* path) ; the saint ' has no time for ' anything but the will of

God. *We* feel that unless we are supported—it doesn't much matter how—we shall be hopelessly unsafe: the saint feels that he is safe *only* when he has no artificial supports whatever; because then he can 'cast all his care upon the Lord,' knowing that the Lord will infallibly care for him. The life of the saint is lived 'in God' (and 'God in him') to such an extent that anything in the nature of an 'artificial support' is immediately perceived and, as immediately, expelled. That is what I mean when I say that the saint has 'no time for' artificial supports, while there is time—plenty of time—for them with us. In fact we make time for them.

Now what is all this about 'artificial supports,' and what do I mean by 'all kinds of influences, some of them extremely worthy'? In answer let it be said at the outset and in general that anything which results from our trying to *measure* perfection is bound to be tainted with what we will call—for want of a better term—'self' (not 'selfishness,' necessarily, but 'nature,' 'humanness,' 'self'). Whenever we judge humanly a thing which in itself is spiritual we are leaving room for 'self'; in so far, therefore, as we use our own terms, set our own standards, apply our own tests, assess at our own valuation, and draw our own conclusions—which is what I mean by 'measuring'—just so far are we laying ourselves open to being side-tracked from the true. (It is understood, of course, that I am talking now of what pertains to the strictly spiritual sphere.)

If we are side-tracked from the true, we are forced on to the avenues of the false; at best we are admitting scope for the 'artificial.' An 'artificial support,' therefore, to our process of reasoning and to whatever

conclusions we finally arrive would be (for example) :
' I must do this penance because Blessed So-and-so
practised it,' or : ' That book on Detachment says that
such-and-such a thing must be given up.' I call these
most worthy motives for action, but not necessarily the
motives which should determine *our particular* action.
The saint—to get back to him—does not try to model
himself on any one follower of Christ, he tries to
re-present the Model in himself ; he tries to be an *alter
Christus*, another Christ, and not another somebody else.
He can follow this terrific vocation only by doing what
he believes to be Christ's wish for *him*—regardless of
what it is for other people. A feeble simile might be
suggested in the colours on the canvas : each is contributing *its* share. That is to say it would be no use
for the vermilion to pretend to the sobriety of burnt
sienna or for the ochre to envy the intensity of chrome ;
each has its proper function ; each must act according
to its nature ; all are doing the same thing, but each
is doing it in a different way—*its* way.

' One of the fathers questioned the great abbot
Nistero, who was a friend of abbot Antony, and said :
" What good work shall I do ? " And he answered :
" All good works are not equal. The Scripture saith
that Abraham was hospitable and God was with him.
That David was humble and God was with him.
What therefore thou findest thy soul desireth in following God, that do, and keep thy heart." ' The quotation
is from *The Sayings of the Fathers ;* I am afraid I
have lost the reference. An even more apt citation
(and one I am able this time to verify) might be taken
from Fr Martindale's book, *The Creative Words of
Christ,* where he says (p. 49) that the ' starry examples
of the saints may trick us into the habit of star-gazing

E

—of imagining ourselves to be, or wishing we were, or giving up hopes of being, something that God never intended for us—for no man is meant to be just any other man . . .'

In that case (it might be urged) why *have* saints ? If we are not meant to imitate them what *are* we to do with them ? The question is a large one and this is hardly the kind of book which is expected to find an answer ; the line of thought, however, which I would suggest to anyone who might be inclined to wonder what saints were *for* would be roughly this : The variety of calls, the variety of penances, the variety of pious practices, *in fact the variety of types of saint*, are all so many pieces of evidence for the fact that *no* walk of life, *no* course of prayer or penance, *no* sincere following of Christ is without its special patron : in other words, we are meant to learn from the diversity of sainthood the unity of our incorporation in Christ.

If, then, we can all be saints, and if some of the people we are mixing with quite possibly *are* saints, where exactly does the difference come in ? If sanctity does not consist in the results achieved, what does it consist in ? Clearly the answer to this last question is that sanctity consists in the continued pressure which the soul brings to bear upon the business of being faithful to grace. Where the difference between heroic holiness and ordinary first-class goodness comes in is not to be gauged by rule of thumb : saints are different to us only in the degree of sensitiveness with which they perceive the calls of grace—and the promptitude with which they respond to them. It does not require another *faculty* so to respond, it merely requires a readier fidelity, a larger generosity ; and, as has been said, this fidelity (or generosity) is made more ready (or more large) when it does not waste time on the ways and means that have 'supported,' however successfully, under other circumstances.

'But surely,' it might be objected, 'this leaves the door open for a rather arbitrary line of conduct ; if what you say is true it seems that the thing to do is, when in doubt, to act on impulse. The saints (on the above theory) were the fortunate ones who happened to have guessed right and jumped quickest.' I would answer this highly legitimate attack by saying that, on the contrary, the saint never acts on impulse, because he tests every inspiration that comes to him. His 'inspirations' have to appear before the bar of reason, and it is a reason moreover which is far more clear-sighted and exacting than the reason which is found in the rest of men. The process is known as the exercise of 'prudence.'[1] Prudence is a cardinal virtue, and its function is discernment ; the more we have of it the better. 'Be not conformed to this world but be reformed in the newness of your mind, that you may prove what is the good, and the acceptable, and the perfect will of God.'[2] Prudence enables us to do that. Prudence was precisely the virtue which was working in Daniel when he ' discerned ' between what of Babylon he would accept and what he would reject.

We talk in a loose sort of way about a saint's 'instinct' . . . about holy people 'getting a *feeling*' about what is of God and what is of the devil. . . .

---

[1] This is prudence in its theological, catechismal, sense. That is to say it is not the same as ' precaution ' ; a man exercises ' precaution ' when he goes out with an umbrella—he need not necessarily be practising the virtue of prudence. Precaution is ' taking care.' ; prudence is ' that which enlightens the mind and points out the most effectual means for carrying out the work of salvation.'

[2] Romans xii, 2.

It would be a mistake (I think) to regard this intuitiveness—except where it is present quite obviously in the form of a miraculous gift from God[1]—as being anything more than the kind of thing which we ourselves possess but which we use more clumsily. The 'intuitions' of a good man are worth following, not because they represent his 'feelings' but because they do *not* represent his feelings—or anyone else's. The 'intuitions' of a good man—and still more of a saint —only *look like* inspirations of the moment because the process of arriving at them has been so rapid. But he has arrived at them only through the use of the same dull unromantic faculty which enables us to arrive at *our* conclusions : the reasoning faculty, the practical judgement. The rapidity, the 'spur of the moment,' is due to the fact that he (the good man, the saint) uses this reasoning faculty more often . . . and is therefore in better practice. Also, as has been suggested above, the saint uses his reasoning faculty more purely and so does not have to spend time in sweeping away secondary motives.

It is because the saints had to 'discern' between different situations that different saints have turned out different from one another. If all situations were spiritually the same, or if all spiritual men were cast in the same mould, there would be no need for the virtue of 'discernment.' But life is not (happily or unhappily) as straightforward as that, and there is no such mass-production in the formation of men's souls —with the result that we *must* decide things, we *must* take steps, we *must* be prepared to strike out lines of

---

[1] St Philip Neri, St John Bosco, St John Baptist Vianney, and many others were quite clearly granted strictly supernatural powers of the kind suggested here ; these saints could ' sense ' good and evil when there were no outward indications whatever.

our own . . . even if they are found to be hard lines. It is not that we are expected to set custom at nought, not that we can expect to enjoy the *rôle* of individualist, not that we must take it upon ourselves to reproach our fellow Christians . . . it is rather that we must place the real things first and put all else in relation to that reality. The essential reality is the will of God. The saint is open to the call of grace (another term for the will of God) however odd it makes him look in his obedience to it. He does not choose to be odd, he takes his oddities in his stride towards God. He knows himself to be a ' pilgrim and a stranger '— and a stranger is nothing if not strange. Like all pilgrims that are foreigners he knows that he belongs elsewhere, and that as long as he is moving towards his goal he can afford to look a fool in the eyes of passers-by. His way towards the goal may be a roundabout way ; he may even feel himself to be the only person on it ; but it is the way, all the same, that leads to the Beloved . . . and in the pin-head summit of the soul he knows it. And as for us (we who are not saints) it is our business to walk in the direction of the saints. And even to walk in their footsteps. But it is not always a wise thing to try and wear their shoes.

Ah, yes, even for us (let alone for the saint) this requires courage. One would hardly expect holiness to come without a struggle. But, for consolation, see what a glorious independence is the outcome of such bravery : ' This is the victory which overcometh the world—our faith.'[1] It may be that we stand by ourselves, but we stand as victors—at all events in the sight of God. Think of the detachment which is the reward of such faith ! The opinions of men are for-

[1] 1 John v, 4.

gotten in listening for the voice of God; human considerations appear *as* human considerations, and are rejected as being not worth while in the light of what alone is lasting in the life of man. Think, again, of the fearlessness which such a faith must bring ! The future, however bleak or fraught with possible mishap, ceases to evoke a tremor in those who live in terms of eternity. The soul becomes majestically free the moment it chooses to follow the lead of God. This courageous freedom is not the power to plan one's life and the strong-mindedness to elbow one's way along the course of it, it is much more the being unafraid to burn our boats, to scrap our self-made rules, to turn our humanly devised and fool-proof systems inside out, to exchange our own ideas on the subject (in other words) for ' a yet more excellent way.'[1] ' That I may be found in Him, not having *my* justice, which is of the law, but that which is of the faith of Jesus Christ, which is of God : justice in faith.'[2]

It is faith, then, in the ' care of God,' trust in the unseen order of His plan, that alone can give to the mind and heart of man that detachment which makes easy the exercise of his practical judgement ; cool thought, distilled as it were in the presence of God and yet not so cool as to grow cold in the waiting, is needed if the soul is to estimate the lengths it is to go in following the calls which it thinks to have come from God. Such at all events was the detachment which ensured the safety of Daniel's decision.

.   .   .   .   .

' *Try*, I beseech thee, thy servants for ten days, and let pulse be given us to eat and water to

---

[1] 1 Corinthians xii, 31.   [2] Philippians iii, 9.

drink . . . he tried them for ten days . . . their faces appeared fairer and fatter than all the children that ate of the king's meat . . . and God gave knowledge and understanding and wisdom to these [the Hebrew] children . . .'

For vindication of a policy can anything be clearer than that ? God, evidently, favours a certain die-hardism when it comes to the keeping of His law ; His favour is shown not by heavenly music but by the very simple and 'natural' phenomenon of a combined increase of weight and diligence in study.

We can picture the genial custodian, Malasar, deal-ing out liberal helpings of pulse day after day and week after week, and wondering why these good-looking young men should be taking their religion so seriously. A crying shame, he would call it, to treat the body in such a way . . . well, piety took different people in different ways . . . and it wasn't for him to criticise, but this sort of thing would not suit *him* . . . and coming from the Jewish aristocracy too, so they said . . . well, he never did.

And all the while, presumably, ' the full portions and the wine that they should drink ' were adequately dealt with in the servants' quarters down below.

CHAPTER IV

DANIEL AND THE KING'S DREAM
(*Daniel ii.*)

i

' In the second year of the reign of Nabuchodonosor, Nabuchodonosor had a dream, and his
spirit was terrified and his dream went out of his
head.'

IN all, Nabuchodonosor reigned forty-three years
(604–561). For some time before his father's death
he had been acting as coadjutor, and it is conjectured
that the ' second year ' refers to the third year of his
actual accession—the Babylonian method of reckoning
being to start from the year following the coronation.
Thus the ' third year ' of the Prophet's training in the
schools might well come before the ' second year ' of
Nabuchodonosor's reign. In which case there is no
difficulty about the order of events as described in this
and the foregoing chapter.[1]

The story of Nabuchodonosor's dream bears a dis-
tinct resemblance to the narrative recorded in
Genesis xli, where another unbelieving sovereign has

[1] But there are many ways of getting round the ' second year '
difficulty ; see the article under *Chronology* in Hastings' *Dictionary
of the Bible*, and also Driver, op. cit., p. 17. In any case it is not
a point that matters very much.

another baffling dream which is revealed by another Hebrew exile. Joseph and Daniel have many points in common : they are alike much sought after on account of their good looks, alike tender-hearted, alike exposed to danger from man and beast, and alike—once vindicated—advanced to the highest offices in the lands of their respective adoption. Daniel (at least so it seems to me) is the happier man of the two ; there is a gaiety about the Prophet that is absent in the Patriarch. Both had much to endure, many deep questions to decide, heavy responsibilities to bear, and the darkest of national issues to face, but one feels that Joseph was a more solemn person from the beginning ; had Joseph dealt with the Egyptians in the spirit that Daniel was to deal with the Chaldeans we should not have had quite such a sombre—or indeed quite such a beautiful—page of Genesis. It is as well also that Daniel and not Joseph is the hero of the Bel and dragon stories or we should never have had such a lighthearted rounding off of the Book in front of us. But this is to begin at the wrong end.

One reason why the king was so much distressed by the dream he had had was that he could not for the life of him remember what it was about. ' Then the king commanded to call together the diviners and magicians . . . so they came and stood before the king.'

We have seen from his building activities that Nabuchodonosor was not a man to waste time (his second palace is said to have been finished within fifteen days from the laying of the foundation stone[1]) ; it is therefore no surprise to us when we learn that as soon as it was day—immediately after the dream in

[1] So, at all events, Berosus as quoted in Driver, xxv.

fact—wise men and sorcerers were sent for to make the matter clear. Doubtless the adjoining academy had often before been made use of by the king, but it is probable that the assistance which it had provided had come chiefly from the faculties of architecture, languages, history and science ; now was the time for testing the more airy branches of the sapiential tree which spread itself unseen in luxuriant growth over the way. Not for nothing would king Nabuchodonosor pay ample stipends to his hired mystics ; the tree would be tested by its fruits . . . and were there no fruit forthcoming, the tree should be cut down.

The sun, then, has scarcely risen, and the air about Babylon is still fresh, when the king comes out on to his balcony and scans with a meditative eye the town, the suburbs, and the many miles of land that he can call his own. Here, on his birthday and on other great days, he has been accustomed to appear in his royal purple and accept the homage of his people. Demonstrations of this kind, however, are absent from his thoughts to-day. All that he wants now is to calm his troubled spirit by looking at a panorama which he has found from experience to be soothing to the nerves. Between the palms and orange-groves he can see the indigo line of horizon and watch the light streaming into his city from the circle of burnished gold that is rising in the blue of a cloudless sky. He feels the breeze of the early morning on his face and neck. He hears the hundred little noises of a big city getting up. In a few minutes the streets will begin to fill with colour and movement ; at present there is only the taking down of shutters, the harnessing of horses, the stretching of awnings over barrows and counters in the bazaar. . . .

Nabuchodonosor's eyes rest on the details of his
own palace grounds before him. He sees what he
expects to see : everything orderly, well kept, decent.
But he sees something else as well, something he has
waited for and which gives him further reason to
congratulate himself on the smooth running of his
household. It is the group of magicians and diviners
that he sees, hurrying across the court between the
palace and the palace gates. From above, and
especially to Nabuchodonosor's night-starved fancy,
these men look indeed like leaves torn by a tempest
from the branches of some exotic growth ; frail old
creatures they are, these sorcerers, fluttering over the
paved courtyard floor, their claret-coloured cloaks
floating and folding in the breeze of haste. Well, if the
tree has been rudely shaken already, it will be shaken
a good deal more in the storm that is to come !

' So they came and stood before the king '—awed,
obsequious, and—if we may be allowed the inference
—not a little apprehensive. Favoured apprentices
stand each behind his master ; there is an impressive
array of phials, crystal globes, astronomical instruments, books, boxes, knives, and charts.[1]

' And the king said to them : I saw a dream, and
being troubled in my mind I know not what I saw.'
The necromancers are faintly relieved : they have the

[1] Babylonia was famed for its magical arts. So much so that
the term ' Chaldean ' came to mean anyone that was skilled in the
occult practices of divination, enchantment, omen-reading, etc.
' Fully one-fourth of the portion of Asshurbanabal's library that has
been discovered consists of omen-tablets of various sizes in which
explanations are afforded of all physical peculiarities to be observed
in animals and men, of natural phenomena, of the position and
movements of the planets and stars, of the incidents and accidents
of public and private life—in short, of all possible occurrences and
situations.' Jastrow, *Religion of Babylonia and Assyria*, p. 406.

science of this sort of thing at their finger-tips ; it
would have been much more awkward if they had
been told to do by magic what the engineers and
architects had been doing by forced labour. One
never knew with Nabuchodonosor . . . he might want
to save money for something or other, and at the same
time continue his geographical experiments with various
local sites ; it would indeed have been upsetting had
the king insisted on a spirit-produced viaduct or a few
more hanging-gardens. But a mere *dream !* Child's
play ! The wise men smile and bow.

' O king, live for ever ; tell to thy servants thy
dream and we will declare the interpretation thereof.'
(But that is precisely the difficulty.) ' The thing,'
says the king, ' is gone out of my mind.'

There is an uncomfortable pause and a general sense
of deadlock.

Then Nabuchodonosor, feeling perhaps somewhat
at a loss—and feeling certainly that if it is the business
of these men to lay bare the occult then one mystery
should be as easy to clear up as another—tries to cut
short the interview with a curt statement of his inten-
tions : the death penalty is pronounced upon failure to
' declare the dream ' and rewards are offered for the
successful solution . . . one or the other, and there
you have it. There is no waiting in the affairs of
Nabuchodonosor ; briskness and efficiency are the
order of the day. But the wise men—justifiably
enough, heaven knows—can hardly let the matter
drop at this particular point in the conversation.
' Let the king tell his servants the dream,' they repeat,
' and we will declare the interpretation of it.'

To do Nabuchodonosor justice we must remember
that he was very much on edge in any case—bad

night, bad dream, no food as yet—so it is not to be
wondered at if he was unable, having heard the wise
men's last remark, to suffer fools with joy. It was not
the smallest use pointing out to Nabuchodonosor that
the function of a ' determiner ' began with finding out
the meaning of dreams and not with finding out the
dreams themselves ; the king was far too angry to
listen to reason. ' I know for certain that you seek
to gain time, since you know that the thing is gone
from me.' And at this stage agitation confuses his
speech because he goes on in rather an inconsequent
way (but perhaps it is the text and not the king that
is at fault in grammatical exactitude) : ' If you tell
me not the dream, there is one sentence concerning
you, that you have also framed a lying interpretation
and full of deceit to speak before me till the time pass
away.' But the sentence that follows is clear enough :
' Tell me the dream that I may know that you also
give a true interpretation thereof.' This is a perfectly
fair way of handling the situation : the diviners '
revelation of the dream would prove the validity of
the interpretation which they were so ready to put
upon it. How would the king otherwise know that
he was not being duped ? And then, on the other
hand : no dream—no further need of diviners. Sim-
plicity itself. But to the wise men the reasoning
appeared unreasonable. And in practice what
the king wanted could not be done. They told
him so.

' Upon hearing this, the king in a fury and in a great
wrath, commanded that all the wise men of Babylon
should be put to death.' How large is the bearing of
this man ! How massive his outlook ! How wholesale
his decrees ! And how horribly cheap is life in the

seventh century B.C. ! ' The decree being gone forth,
the wise men were slain.'¹

ii

It is now that the gentle, reticent Daniel is thrust
upon the stage ; for he, along with the other wise men
who shared the king's hospitality, fell under the decree.
So did the three Israelites, his companions. The
students' wing in the great collegiate building was
to be swept clean. And one wonders whether it was the
first time in the memory of contemporary Babylon
that such a thing had happened.

> ' And when Arioch had told the matter to
> Daniel, Daniel went in and desired of the king
> that he would give him time to resolve the question
> and declare it to the king.'

It seems that in spite of Nabuchodonosor's haste to
do away with the magicians, Daniel's appeal for more
time was listened to without a murmur. It may be

¹ Isaias's chapter xlvii (written a hundred years earlier) is particularly interesting in the light of the above. He is referring to the
final collapse of Babylon in Baltassar's reign and not to the years
immediately before us ; the insistence on Babylon's sorceries, however, as being mostly responsible for her downfall is appropriate to
the present passages. If Babylon had ' hearkened to the voice of
the Lord ' instead of listening, earlier on, to the vain incantations of
the magicians the Chaldean Empire might not have crumbled so
ignominiously. ' All things are come upon thee,' says Isaias,
' because of the multitude of thy sorceries, and for the great hardness of thy enchanters . . . thy wisdom and thy knowledge, this
hath deceived thee. And thou hast said in thy heart : I am, and
there is no other . . . stand now with thy enchanters and with the
multitude of thy sorceries in which thou hast laboured from thy
youth, if so be it may profit thee anything, or if thou mayest become
stronger . . . let now the astrologers stand and save thee, they that
gazed at the stars and counted the months . . . behold they are
as stubble, *fire hath burnt them, they shall not deliver themselves from
the power of the flames.*'

that the introduction of quite a new deity into the affairs of the king's soul brought some ray of hope that the riddle might yet be solved. At any rate the destruction of *some* of the wise men would be delayed until the morrow.[1] With this encouraging news Daniel joined his friends, ' and he told the matter to Ananias and Misael and Azarias to the end that they should ask mercy of the face of the God of heaven concerning this secret, and that Daniel and his companions might not perish with the rest of the wise men of Babylon.'

The Hebrew youths would have begun their prayer towards the evening of that same eventful day. (Even if the other wise men *were* slain it would not have taken all day to do it, and there is no reason to believe that Daniel's petition had to go from one office to another before it finally received the king's attention. So it was almost certainly the same day ; although in *v.* 19—which follows the passage just quoted—we read that the mystery was revealed to the Prophet in ' *a* night-vision '—suggesting *any* night. But it is only some texts that leave it open even to this extent ; our version says simply ' a vision in the night.')

Daniel leading, the four young men would have mounted the stairs that opened out on to the flat sun-baked roof, each one thinking in his heart that it was probably for the last time. Apart from ' holy ground ' —the temple precincts and so forth—the roof is the place for prayer in the East. Here on the roof of a very unprayerful palace, high up above the level of

---

[1] It is our text only that says, as quoted above, ' The decree being gone forth the wise men *were* slain ' ; other versions have ' that the wise men *should be* slain,' so it is possible that Daniel's plea benefited the magicians as well as himself and his Hebrew companions.

the other houses in the city and with their faces towards
Jerusalem, the exiled Hebrews would have begun
their prayer for light. From where they knelt, under
the shelter of an awning of twisted rushes, they would
have been able to see little more than the sky and the
stretch of hot brown tableland that came to meet it
in a belt of quivering mist at the horizon. They
would have had little to distract them from their
devotions for even the noises of the street would
hardly have reached them there. By this time in the
afternoon the main rush of traffic would have been
over and the people of Babylon would have begun to
think of their evening's entertainment. There was at
least one advantage (so the Hebrews would have
reflected) in being housed at the king's pleasure : you
were not overlooked by your neighbours. The roof-
life of Babylon—not one of the more respectable signs
of the city's animation—must have been in striking
contrast with the purpose for which this particular
roof was being used to-night. Somehow or other
roof-gardens tend to grow poisonous grasses, and if
this is so to-day it was certainly the same in the
Babylon of the seventh century B.C.

Daniel and his friends had not finished their suppli-
cations when the sun sank beneath the sky-line and
when the rough-cast parapet in front of them was
edged with gold. Darkness, in fact, found them still
at it. And it would seem from the text that they were
fasting in addition to keeping vigil because there is no
mention of an interruption until the ' vision in the
night ' was granted. One wonders if Daniel received
his revelation awake or asleep ; there is no possible
means of knowing.

' Then was the mystery revealed to Daniel by a vision

in the night ; and Daniel blessed the God of heaven.'
After which follow four verses giving the Prophet's
prayer of thanksgiving. Thereupon events moved
quickly : Daniel sought out Arioch at once (dragging
him out of bed, it seems, and forcing him into a suit
of clothes) ; an audience was fixed with the king for
as early an hour as possible ; Arioch ' in haste brought
in Daniel to the king.'

' The king said to Daniel whose name was Baltassar :
Thinkest thou indeed that thou canst tell me the dream
that I saw and the interpretation thereof ? And Daniel
made answer before the king, and said : The secret
that the king desireth to know, none of the wise men
or the philosophers or the diviners or the soothsayers
can declare to the king. But there is a God in heaven
That revealeth mysteries, Who hath shown to thee,
O king Nabuchodonosor, what is to come to pass in
the latter times. Thy dream and the visions of thy
head upon thy bed are these ' : And here we imagine
Daniel taking a deep breath before launching out into
the particular ' mystery ' that the ' God in heaven '
has revealed to him. Before going on to examine the
dream and what it meant there are one or two minute
points which perhaps deserve comment. In the first
place Nabuchodonosor's question seems to be more
than a formal opening to the conversation ; it suggests
that he had quite given up the hopes which he had
entertained the day before ; and that in any case
one so young as Daniel—for all his triumphs on the
platform of a month or two ago—was not very likely
to meet the difficulty. Daniel's answer to the king is
also worthy of notice : he acknowledged at once that
he had got nothing to contribute in the way of a solution, ' but there is a God in heaven That revealeth

mysteries . . .' It is a brave proclamation.[1] Incidentally we notice that Daniel made it perfectly clear that
though *he*—left to himself—would never have made
anything of the business, yet at the same time there
was nobody else in the kingdom who could ! ' None
of the wise men or the philosophers or the diviners or
soothsayers . . .' yes, it was just as well that the king
should be made amply aware of that. But as a matter
of fact, of course, the king knew it only too well
already.

Then (while Nabuchodonosor was still wondering
how it was that a Hebrew should boast of his God
while Chaldeans made excuses for theirs) came the
dream.

The dream-portion of this chapter (ii) occupies a
comparatively large place : 15 verses out of the 49.
The reader is inclined to feel perhaps that the dream,
when it finally stands revealed, is ever so slightly
disappointing. One would somehow like it to transcend
history in flights of mystical theology ; one would wish
that it contained the sum of Hebrew spirituality—
and that Nabuchodonosor would be converted by it ;
one would like it to have some bearing upon the exiled
Jews in Babylon ; or one would be pleased to have a
picture of the Christ Who was to come. . . .

Well, anyway, the revelation took the following
form : the king was told that he had seen in his sleep
a great statue ; the head had been of gold, the breast
and arms of silver ; the body had been made of brass,
the legs of iron, the feet partly of iron, partly of clay.
Then had come violent action into the dream, and a

---

[1] And is an echo, again, of Joseph's self-deprecatory expressions ;
see Genesis xl, 8, and xli, 16. Seeing where these protestations were
made—in the heart of disbelief—we marvel at the readiness of
Joseph and Daniel.

great boulder, ' cut without hands out of a mountain,'
had fallen and crushed the feet of the statue. The
figure had thereupon crashed to the ground and
crumbled to bits. The boulder had become a vast
mountain, large enough to ' fill the whole earth.'
This is how Daniel explained the dream : the gold
head, he said, was Nabuchodonosor himself (together
with the kingdom which was to reach its apogee under
his rule) ; Nabuchodonosor's dynasty would be
succeeded by an inferior one ; a third would follow
—of baser metal still—which would be of universal
sway, but which would exercise its power ruthlessly ;
the very rigidity of this kingdom would prove its
weakness. God would then set up a Kingdom which
would be greater than all these kingdoms, and of this
last Kingdom there would be no end. ' And the
dream is true,' said Daniel at the close of his explanation, ' and the interpretation thereof is faithful.'

' Then Nabuchodonosor fell on his face '—so the
text runs on—' and worshipped Daniel.' *Daniel !*
The Prophet must have wasted no time in correcting
the misplaced adoration because we find in the next
verse that the king is, quite properly, attributing all
power and wisdom to the God of Israel.[1]

[1] There exists (I think in the Accademia at Venice) an
indifferent picture illustrating the dramatic finish to Daniel's
interview with the king. The artist, whose name I have succeeded
in forgetting, shows Nabuchodonosor in the act of sliding from his
throne, so eager is he to worship—be it the Prophet or the Prophet's
God. With equal earnestness sinister figures are seen to be making
off in the direction of the marble steps that lead, doubtless, to the
palace gates. The artist has—incidentally and evidently—followed
the reading that allows the sorcerers a temporary reprieve. Daniel
the while—serene, confident, slightly flushed and presumably
wearing a wig—looks down upon Nabuchodonosor's golden crown
with an expression that is obviously charged with the deepest
meaning. One feels that the full significance of the Prophet's gaze
is locked in the painter's breast. The picture is an interesting one;
it quite definitely ' tells a story.'

Daniel is then advanced to high station, is given presents, and is summoned to live in the king's palace. The three Israelites, Daniel's friends, are at the Prophet's request 'placed over the works of the province of Babylon.' What precisely the 'works of the province of Babylon' were, and what being placed over them involved, we do not know. It seems fairly certain that Daniel became responsible for the administration of the Babylonian area in the capacity of—what, in classical times, would be known as ' Prefect '—and that the posts given to the three young men were in some way related to that. But it is not a point of great moment. What were the feelings of the native officials about all this ? How did the other ' wise men ' in the palace—if indeed there remained any after yesterday's slaughter—view the promotion of their juniors ? The Bible is silent on these questions, but for answer we can make, I think, a pretty fair guess.

iii

A few words had better be said about the application of the dream and its bearing upon subsequent history. The student who wishes to go into the matter thoroughly will find an ample literature at his disposal.[1] I attempt no more than the merest summing up. And for those whose interest lies more in the personalities of Daniel's story than in the historical value of

---

[1] The authorities that state their views most clearly, though the views do not in every case agree, are (to my mind and to my confessedly limited range of reading) : Driver, op. cit., xi, 17, 98–102 ; Deane, op. cit., pp. 58–61 ; Kelly, *Lectures on the Book of Daniel*, pp. 33–48. Fr Hugh Pope unfortunately does not go into the question. In citing the above-mentioned names I am considering, of course, only the *historical* issue, not the moral conclusions that may be derived from the dream and its explanation.

his predictions and the morals that can be drawn from them, this section can conveniently be omitted.

First of all as regards history. The essential material could be adequately dealt with on the back of an envelope ; it will be necessary, however, to amplify the four key-statements ever so slightly in order to show how apt were the symbols to the four different dynasties involved. Daniel, it should be noticed, names one kingdom only—Nabuchodonosor's—leaving to posterity the work of putting labels on the rest.

The gold head, then, denotes Chaldea at its best. Babylon, at the time when Nabuchodonosor is dreaming his dream, has greater opportunities than any other unbelieving nation of coming to the true faith. The prophets of Israel have been sent to her ; her people, though misguided and polytheistic, are receptive to the things of the spirit ; her king is a genius and—after a fashion—just ; her industries flourish ; her children multiply ; her borders are enlarged from year to year. ' Golden ' are Babylon's chances—if only she will grasp at them. But she won't, with the result that the second kingdom, the kingdom of silver, takes Babylon's place. This new power is variously taken to mean either the Medes by themselves, or the combined rule of the Medes and Persians. More probable, it seems to me, is the first alternative. Media lay somewhat north of Babylon and had for generations past been a cause of harassing anxiety to whichever of the two great nations happened to be in the ascendancy at the time— Assyria or Chaldea. It was not until about 600 B.C. that the Medes came really to the fore in international affairs. Cyaxares (624–584) was the first to mould the scattered pugnacious people into a responsible nation ; it was under him that the Medes (assisted by their

temporary allies the Chaldeans) reduced the power of
Nineveh until that city—and ultimately the whole
Assyrian Empire—fell. After Cyaxares came Astyages,
who was obliged, by the desertion of his army, to yield
his empire into the hands of Cyrus. This was in 549.

So if the second kingdom represents that of Media,
the third must denote that of Persia. This is the
kingdom of brass. The extent of its sway is described
as being ' over all the earth,' and this is hardly an
exaggeration when we consider that the then known
world became almost entirely Persian territory. Asia
Minor and Egypt (this embraces Palestine, Chaldea,
what had been Assyria, and in fact the whole of Western
Asia) were, by 527 B.C., paying tribute to the Great
Cyrus's successor, Cambyses. Cambyses died in 522
and was succeeded by Darius the Great who is also
referred to as Hystaspes. This Darius is not the Darius
the Mede who is mentioned by Daniel later on in the
story. Daniel's Darius was appointed by Cyrus and
may possibly be identified with Astyages's successor,
Cyaxares II ; we must deal with him when we come
to the part he plays in Chapter V and after.

The fourth, or iron, kingdom is taken to be the
Macedonian Empire founded by Alexander the Great.
Its power is crushing and unyielding but, being mixed
with a different and a weaker material, is unable to
support itself : division proves its undoing. This
unhappy fusion of incompatible elements alludes to
the way in which the Greek Empire was to be parcelled
out by Alexander's successors. The Macedonian or
Greek Empire split up into two separate dynasties :
the Seleucidæ and the Ptolemies ; of these the stronger
was that of Seleucus and so is to be taken as the
' iron ' of Nabuchodonosor's dream, while the ' clay '

represents Ptolemy Lagi's kingdom in Egypt. The stone which Nabuchodonosor had seen falling upon the feet of the statue is, as has been said, the beginnings of the rule of God. God's Kingdom was to be established when the image had fallen and when the component elements had been scattered like chaff before the wind. It is conjectured that the fall of the ' stone ' alludes to the time of Antiochus Epiphanes (A.D. 164-175), whose fall was to mark the introduction of a new Sovereignty.[1]

Before passing on to what I regard as the more important aspect of Daniel's revelation—namely, the practical moral application—I must interject a possible variation to the historical allusions accounted for above. Which is that the Roman and not the Grecian Empire is represented by the iron and clay feet of the statue. It is this view that is put forward, and defended with some warmth, by William Kelly in his book already referred to, *Lectures on the Book of Daniel*. In some ways it is a more satisfactory theory than the other—especially since it brings the fall of the last

---

[1] A statue of Antiochus Epiphanes was erected upon the sacred altar in Jerusalem during that king's scoundrelly reign. A strong tradition has assigned to this act the implications contained in the ' abomination of desolation which is spoken of in Daniel the Prophet ' (see Matthew xxiv, 15), where Our Lord is referring to a sign that is to warn Jerusalem of its approaching destruction. The relevant passages in Daniel are ix, 27 ; xi, 31 ; xii, 11. If, however, the profanation which is meant by the ' abomination ' refers to some act of sacrilege *subsequent* to the Antiochus Epiphanes outrage (as those would hold who follow the theory which will be discussed in the next paragraph), then some new ' abomination ' must be sought : some act connected with Roman rule. The introduction of Roman standards into the Temple and the erection of Hadrian's statue in the Holy Place are alike events which took place *after* the fall of Jerusalem. So they can hardly be said to be ' signs ' of the Holy City's destruction.

It is the opinion of Lagrange that Our Lord's words refer to the acts of sacrilege which were to be performed after His death when the Zealots took possession of the Temple.

dynasty nearer to the Birth of Christ—but it means
that you have to group the Medes and the Persians
together and call them both the ' silver ' layer in the
statue's composition. If Rome *is* the feet of the statue,
then all I ask is that some more satisfactory explanation
of the ' clay ' be given us than that which has so far
been advanced by the champions of the theory.
Fortunately we may preserve an open mind on the
subject.

Now for the more general application of the dream :
the meaning which it must have for others besides
those peoples who rose and fell before the coming of the
Kingdom ' made without hands.' Surely we do not
have to look far ; the lesson of Nabuchodonosor's
dream has been repeated throughout the centuries ;
it is our fault if we have not learnt it. Again, it could
be told on a single page.

The truth that the iron rule ultimately defeats itself
is as neglected now as it was in the time of Daniel—and
after ; modern civilisation is in danger of going the
same way as did Chaldea, Media, Persia, and Greece.
Ever since the days of Elias the Thesbite, Israel had
been warned that God was not in the earthquake and
the storm ;[1] the dream of Nabuchodonosor was but
a repetition of the warning. If even in the Old Testament we are told that the acts of God are done gently,
we are told it with far greater emphasis in the New.
The similes used by Our Lord for His Kingdom, for
the action of grace in the soul, for the Church's growth,
are all of them—as is the very life of Christ Himself—
expressive of a tempered, flexible, living and, if
necessary, a *yielding* power. The training which we
undergo is not *forced* upon us ; rather it is, in its

[1] 3 Kings xix, 11.

literal sense, an education—a 'leading out': an eduction from 'darkness into His marvellous Light.' Our Lord prefers that we should be leavened from within rather than that we should be moulded from without. In the Old Testament we were clay in the potter's hand,[1] in the New Testament we are bread, we are branches, we are members of a living Body. Our Lord tells us, further, where this process of 'education' is to be found and, though He is speaking to us in parables, one feels that His similes are so chosen as to bear out even this minor point: we work in vineyards and not in distilleries; we take our lesson from the field and not from the barrack square. The parade ground (and we who are 'soldiers of Christ' might have expected some such simile) is evidently too hard and flat a place for the cultivation of the 'seed which is the word of God.' Rigid methods, cast-iron legislation, dead-level standards are not, if we examine it, God's way. Where the spirit of God is, there is life. We have 'highways and hedges,' not subways and railings of iron. One of the differences between God-made and man-made works is that whatever life the latter seem to possess is at once ephemeral and heartless. Progress—if by that we mean one invention following on top of another—is a thing of fits and starts and halts. The ordering of God, on the other hand, 'worketh all things sweetly,' and is gradual in the unfolding of its course.[2] Ivy, given time, will outlast the wall on which it grows; cement will yield, eventually, to dripping water; trees will be standing when the last telegraph-pole has fallen into the grass

[1] See Jeremias xviii.
[2] 'Wisdom reacheth from end to end mightily, and ordereth all things sweetly' (Wisdom viii, 1).

by the roadside. The Laws of God—whether of nature or of grace—are essential and elemental, and are therefore *alive ;* they adapt themselves, they assimilate to themselves, they impart, they yield, they attract, they reject—in a word, they were made for living men.[1] Thus even where, in the Gospel, Our Lord chooses for His analogue a lifeless thing He seems to press it to a living use. Take, for instance, the ' net which was cast into the sea,' and to which He compares the Kingdom of God on earth. How perfectly does this metaphor act as a companion-picture to Nabuchodonosor's statue ; they form a study in contrasts. The strength of the net is the strength that must know how to ' give ' ; the net must take the strain of the forces that are opposed to it ; the net must be strong enough to let itself be bent and twisted into every kind of unlikely shape and yet retain the power of getting back again into its original form.[2] It was precisely because the nations mentioned in Nabuchodonosor's dream were not net-like that they were doomed to failure. They broke because they could not bend. It is precisely because the dictator-ruled nations of to-day are not net-like—*and* (but this is obvious) because they recognise neither Him Whose net it is nor the Fisherman at Rome who controls it from the Barque of Peter—that they will go the way of the Chaldeans, the Medes, the Persians, and the Greeks. The attempt on

[1] Mgr Knox, in his book *The Mystery of the Kingdom*, writes as follows : ' The Jew thinks of it [the kingdom] as a sudden violent upheaval, a catastrophe of history ; Our Lord teaches that it will be a growth, gradual though it be rapid, akin in its methods of its accomplishment to all that we know of organic growth in nature. . . . Silently through the centuries the supernatural miracle has worked, like nature's miracle of fermentation ' (pp. 28–9).

[2] See Maturin, *Studies on Parables*, p. 85.

the part of contemporary governments to standardise education, the family, employments, and pleasures, will, if successful, more than merely stereotype humanity—it will sterilise it.

.   .   .   .   .

The Kingdom of God, the element struck off ' without hands ' from the matrix mountain, is endowed with the might of One Whose ' power shall be from sea to sea, and from the rivers even unto the ends of the earth.'[2] The strength of this Ruler is such that He was able to say : ' Learn of Me for I am meek and humble of heart.'[3] This was He, moreover, Whose very name means ' God the Mighty,' and of Whom Isaias prophesied that He should ' sit upon the throne of David to strengthen it.'[4] And the way in which this power of His shall be revealed is told for us—again from the Prophet Isaias—' The bruised reed He shall not break, and the smoking flax He shall not quench ; He shall bring forth judgement unto truth.'[5] Whatever the power of earthly kingdoms, God's Household is not to be ruled with the rod of iron. If we think otherwise then are we Boanerges, ' sons of thunder,' not knowing ' of what spirit we are.'[6]

iv

For a time at least, and under pressure from Daniel, the king seems to have favoured belief in the One True God. But beyond the single hint of change of attitude which we get from Nabuchodonosor's ' verily

[2] Zacharias ix, 10. [3] Matthew xi, 29.
[4] Isaias ix, 7. [5] Isaias, xlii, 2.
[6] Cf. Luke ix, 54, 55.

your God is the God of gods '—in the plural—we do not find that the dream had any really transforming effect. And it is nowhere claimed that outside the king's palace any more momentous consequences were forthcoming than those we have already considered : the promotion to high offices of Daniel and his friends. It has been for posterity to benefit by Nabuchodonosor's dream ; God never wastes His revelation ; the Word is living ' and profitable unto many.'

CHAPTER V

THE INCIDENT OF THE FIERY FURNACE
(*Daniel iii.*)

i

'King Nabuchodonosor made a statue of gold of sixty cubits high and six cubits broad, and he set it up in the plain of Dura of the province of Babylon.'

IT was probably some time after his dream that Nabuchodonosor decided to build himself a gold colossus on the plains of Dura. There is no direct indication in the text as to when this new venture was undertaken, but if we may judge from the opening verse of the next chapter (ch. iv, which is, for various reasons which are not worth going into here, considered by the experts to be linked, chronologically, to the chapter we are at present investigating) which says that the king was 'at rest in his house and flourishing' when he turned his attention from war to worship, we can assume that the 'fiery furnace' incident took place between the twentieth and the thirtieth years of his reign. The Septuagint has, as a prefix to this chapter, the words 'in the eighteenth year,' but this is taken to be an addition. The golden image, whatever it was meant to represent in the way of actual likeness, was, as we shall see from the story, a representation of

Nabuchodonosor's theological opinions. And his
interest in theology, it should be noted, began only
when he ' was at rest in his house '—and free from the
anxieties of war [1] Before about 584 B.C. Nabuchodonosor would still have been rather too closely
involved in foreign politics to allow of the predication
' flourishing ' and ' rest.' Jerusalem did not finally
yield to his troops until the year 586, and for the twenty
years previous to the Holy City's fall Nabuchodonosor
had been busy with other nations besides that of Israel ;
Egypt, parts of Arabia, the land of Phœnicia (with its
long-drawn-out siege of Tyre), had each to be dealt
with in turn ; while the temporary good relations that
existed between Chaldea and the Medes required the
king's attention no less. Thus it was during the
peaceful period of his reign that Nabuchodonosor was
able to bequeath to posterity, in the form of an inscription, the intelligence that he enjoyed ' empire over
multitudes.' ' For thy glory,' he said, addressing himself to his favourite god, Marduk, ' I have made a
house . . . may its memorials be augmented.' Is the
image on Dura, one wonders, among these ' memorials '?
Or is Nabuchodonosor's statue a gigantic replica, as
some have suggested, of the king himself ? Alas, we
have no possible means of finding out.

As regards the construction of the image and the
locality in which it stood we have more to go upon
than might have been expected. If the methods were
employed which are indicated by Isaias and Jeremias
for the making of idols[2] then the body of the monument

---

[1] Deane, op. cit., is interesting on this point (pp. 62–4). He
differs, incidentally, from Driver as to the nature of the image
which Nabuchodonosor erected.

[2] Isaias xl, 19 ; Jeremias x, 9.

would have been of cedar- or palm-wood, and only the surface of gold. The amount of gold-plating used in this instance must have been considerable ; sixty cubits equals ninety feet. The width of the statue (six cubits) is in curious disproportion to its height : one would have expected a statue of such a size to have been broader than nine feet. But perhaps it was more of a ' needle ' than a statue. Perhaps it showed only a figure at the summit—like the Nelson Column in Trafalgar Square. Perhaps, like the Albert Memorial, the figure only was of metal, and . . . but perhaps I had better go on to the next point.

There are three possible ' plains of Dura.' The most likely site is a level piece of ground six miles south of Babylon. The whole of this country is, as I have suggested before, as flat as a Hobbema landscape. There is one particular stretch, however, which appears to have been artificially levelled ; in the middle of this there exists to this day a forty-five-foot-square brick emplacement ; it is conjectured by Professor Oppert to be the pedestal belonging to Nabucho-donosor's statue ; the existing structure measures twenty feet deep. The name of the place is now ' Duoir.'

When we consider that the top of the monument stood 110 feet above the ground (the nave of Westminster Abbey is, externally, 102 feet high) and that it was almost the only object to catch the sun in a completely featureless district, we are not surprised to learn that Nabuchodonosor's gilded obelisk was visible within a radius of a dozen miles. And *easily* visible, therefore, from the roof-tops of the Babylon palaces. In fact it must have looked a fine sight in the early morning, its pedestal shrouded in a soft veil of mist and its crown gleaming in the first rays of a new-born day.

> ' Then Nabuchodonosor sent to call together the nobles, the magistrates, and the judges, the captains, the rulers, and governors, and all the chief men of the provinces, to come to the dedication of the statue which king Nabuchodonosor had set up. . . . And they stood before the statue which king Nabuchodonosor had set up.'

Without delaying to go into the distinctions between the above-mentioned offices we may merely note that, of course, the summons included the three Hebrew overseers, Sidrach, Misach, and Abdenago. But it did *not*, apparently, include Daniel. In fact where *was* Daniel in all this ? Surely he would have had something to say to the king's purpose of building an image at all—let alone to the decree that required attendance at the dedication service ? Seeing that the king had already confessed to the God of Israel, this new building venture of his must have shocked his Hebrew friends exceedingly . . . and the one person who might have been expected to raise his voice in legitimate protest —Daniel—is silent ! One explanation that is given us for the Prophet's aloofness from the whole affair is that his position at court was of such an exceptional nature that he was not subject to the decree (and that, having more serious things to worry about, he, presumably, had no notion as to what was going on). This view can *hardly* be accepted. It seems far more likely, in view of the fact that the narrative leaves his name out of account altogether, that at the time of the decree's promulgation Daniel was, and had been for some quite considerable period, ' on circuit.' I say

' for some quite considerable period ' because, though Nabuchodonosor may well have rushed through the building of his monument, the project can scarcely have been a matter of a few days—or even weeks. The most remote provinces had to be ' circularised ' ; governors and satraps had to arrange for ' locum ' administration ; complicated journeys had to be planned and undertaken. . . . No—it would seem that Nabuchodonosor, foreseeing the Prophet's absence from Babylon for some months (and thinking that the Hebrew party among his ministers was powerless without its leader) made plans which he knew would have been resented—if not prevented—by his friend. He then took care to send no messengers to that part of the Empire where Daniel happened at the time to be representing him.

ii

If the fiery furnace story contains no mention of Daniel, why (it might reasonably be objected) bother about it ? I would answer that though this book is meant to give Daniel's life (if it gives anybody's), there are at the same time plenty of things in his Book which, though they have no direct bearing upon the central figure, may profitably be touched upon by his biographer. And even if the fiery furnace incident does not throw much light on the Prophet it throws plenty of light—albeit a somewhat ruddy light—on Nabuchodonosor. It also lights up the three young Jews who up till now have been walking rather in the shadow of their leader. In any case Daniel thought the story worth recording, so why, in the name of Daniel, should not I ?

. . . . . .

'Then the nobles, the magistrates, etc. . . .
were gathered together to come to the dedication
of the statue which king Nabuchodonosor had
set up.'

Suppose we are among the guests at the Dedication.
For some days the city has been getting more and
more crowded : unusual uniforms have been seen in
the streets ; strange accents have been heard at the
theatre and in the baths ; money has circulated
generously, wine has flowed freely, song has echoed
over the waters of the Euphrates. Babylon has
enjoyed getting ready for the feast. Last night chains
of coloured lamps were seen suspended among the trees
of Nabuchodonosor's hanging-gardens ; this morning
banners hang from every window—whether of palace,
of mansion, or of single-roomed abode. Sacred emblems
are displayed over every door ; effigies, in miniature,
of Nabuchodonosor's obelisk are on sale behind every
counter and on every stall and itinerant tray in
Babylon. To-night, when the big function of the day
is over, there will be music, supper-parties, performing
animals, displays of one kind or another (all that goes,
in fact, to what to-day we call the 'cabaret'), and—
dear to the people's heart—numberless speeches.
And all this can be enjoyed, during these warm evenings
of Babylon's season, in the open air and under the
royal purple of a starry sky. Yes, it is very pleasant
indeed. For those who wish it, furthermore (one was
forgetting), there is always the temple of Bel ; that,
like the temple of Marduk, is open to any who might
wish to come.

'And they stood before the statue which king
Nabuchodonosor had set up. Then a herald cried

with a loud voice : To you it is commanded, O nations, tribes, and languages, that in the hour that you shall hear the sound of the trumpet, and of the flute and of the harp, and of the sackbut, and of the psaltery, and of the symphony, and of all kind of music, ye fall down and adore the statue which king Nabuchodonosor has set up. But if any man shall not fall down and adore, he shall the same hour be cast into a furnace of burning fire.'

What a scene it must have been—out there on the sunbaked plain of Dura ! With the helmets and breast-plates and spears, with the women's ornaments, and the horses' harness, with the ' trumpets' and the ' sackbuts ' and the ' psaltery ' and every kind of ' instrument of music,' all glittering—like the great gold ornament itself—in the blazing glare of the midday sun.[1] And then the herald's pronouncement —spoken in clear-cut tones through a silver mouth-piece, every syllable crisp and unmistakable in the untroubled air. . . .

' But if any man shall *not* fall down and adore . . .' Ah, so the king is not so certain after all ! There are some present, evidently, whose attitude towards the idol is still a matter of speculation. Is it the Jews whom Nabuchodonosor has in mind ? Or is it the

---

[1] The ' sackbut ' (heavenly name !) was a small triangular instrument with four strings ; it is said to have been of Syrian origin. This harp-like sackbut of ancient usage is not to be confused with the sackbut of the Middle Ages, which was a wind instrument with a pump or slide—like a trombone. The nearest thing to a ' psaltery ' would be the Arabic *santir*, a stringed instrument which is played with a plectrum ; the *santir* is still to be heard in Egypt. The ' symphony ' is nothing more nor less than the bagpipe !

votaries of other gods besides him to whom honour is being paid to-day ?[1]

.   .   .   .   .

Well, the sequel we know. From our nursery days this episode in Holy Scripture has been familiar enough : how the signal was given and, with a mighty crash of sound, ' all kind of music ' struck out at once ; how—with the exception of three chosen souls—all that vast concourse of men and women bowed down dutifully and worshipped the idol which Nabuchodonosor had set up ; how it was reported to the king that the Hebrew ministers had refused to obey the edict ; how the king, with a tremendous show of passion (but secretly, I think, relieved that it was only three that had refused—and they foreigners), at first interviewed and at last condemned the delinquents to the death of burning. . . . It is a grand tale, let us pause here and see how the Scripture tells it.

' Behold our God Whom we worship,' is the terrific boast of Sidrach, Misach, and Abdenago, ' is able to save us from the furnace of the burning fire, and to deliver us out of thy hand, O King. *But if He will not*,' they go on—and I am not sure that this is not even more brave a statement than the last—' be it known to thee, O King, that *we will not worship thy gods nor the golden statue which thou hast set up*.' The God of Israel is all-powerful, He *can* extinguish flames—as He can

---

[1] Deane makes out a very good case for the theory that Nabuchodonosor, in pressing this image upon the Babylonians, was doing something which was exceedingly unpopular ; he was changing (so Deane) the whole course of traditional Chaldean worship. If this was so then we get still another view of Nabuchodonosor, and a host of questions present themselves. To go into the possibilities of this theory would take us out of the compass of so very amateurish a work as is this present volume. But see Deane, op. cit., pp. 65 ff.

wipe out nations; whether He *will*, in this given instance, see fit to do so, O King, it is not for us to say . . . but in any case we have no intention of paying homage to His enemies. ' Then was Nabuchodonosor filled with fury, and the countenance of his face was changed against Sidrach, Misach, and Abdenago,'— which proves, to my mind, that his anger was only feigned the first time; *now* he feels he has been insulted —' and he commanded that the furnace should be heated seven times more than it had been accustomed to be heated; and he commanded the strongest men that were in his army [!] to bind the feet of Sidrach, Misach, and Abdenago, and to cast them into the furnace of burning fire.'

So high was the ' burning fire ' piled up that the men who had the grisly task of throwing the bound figures into the flames were themselves scorched to death in the process. Mention is made of a curious detail in connexion with the fulfilling of the king's sentence: the three Jews were thrown in ' with their coats and their caps and their shoes and their garments.' Though Daniel was not present at the attempted butchery, one realises that he got the story at first hand; the Jews, who gave him an account of their adventures some time later, would still have been resentful of the wanton waste which the Chaldeans had displayed. Earnest commentators see in this act of wrapping coats and flowing mantles round the bodies of the convicted an attempt to render them more liable to burning. If so, why the ' shoes ' and ' caps ' as well? To me it would seem more reasonable to believe that the cloaks, caps, shoes, and so on were required to be thrown in along with their owners—' required,' I mean, by Providence—so that (73 verses lower down) it could

be said—and recognised by all the judges present—
that 'not a hair of their head had been singed *nor
their garments altered* nor the smell of the fire passed
on them.'

No sooner had they fallen into 'the midst of the
furnace of burning fire' than the three erstwhile
ministers of the crown 'walked in the flame praising
God and blessing the Lord.' The next nineteen verses
(26–45) give the words of their prayer ; the prayer is,
as one would expect it to be, a pæan of the most
magnificent praise. The Protestant Version leaves it
out.

' And the flame mounted up above the furnace nine
and forty cubits ' (compare this with the sixty cubits
of the idol and the 102 feet of Westminster Abbey),
' but the Angel of the Lord went down with Azarias
and his companions into the furnace, and drove the
flame of the fire out of the furnace, and made the midst
of the furnace like the blowing of a wind bringing
dew ; and the fire touched them not at all, nor troubled
them, nor did them any harm.' Can anything be more
winning than this (obviously eye-witnessed) account ?
In the midst of their prayers the Jewish youths measure
up the height of the flames : ' Forty-nine cubits—a
record ! ' As they sing, again, ' an Angel of the Lord '
comes among them and drives away the flames as a
man might shoo away his neighbour's chickens. And
then that soft, beautiful phrase, ' like the blowing of a
wind bringing dew . . .' Prayers, flames, Angels,
cooling breezes . . . the Hebrews are alive to everything that is going on around them. They break out
again into the praises of the Lord ! This time it is the
' Benedicite,' which is an even longer hymn of praise
than the one they have just been singing. They must

have been left in the furnace for some quite considerable time. The 'Benedicite' occupies thirty-eight
verses (52–90); the Protestant Version leaves this
out also.

' Then Nabuchodonosor the king was astonished, and
rose up in haste and said to his nobles : Did we not
cast three men bound into the midst of the fire ? They
answered the king and said : True, O King. He
answered and said : Behold, I see four men loose and
walking in the midst of the fire, and there is no hurt
in them ; and the form of the fourth is like the Son of
God.[1] Then Nabuchodonosor the king came to the
door of the burning fiery furnace and said : Sidrach,
Misach, and Abdenago, ye servants of the most high
God, go ye forth and come.' (Other versions have for
this ' come forth and come hither.') ' And immediately Sidrach, Misach, and Abdenago went out from
the midst of the fire.' After which followed the public
acknowledgement on the part of the assembled nobles
that certainly the Hebrews *had* been miraculously
preserved—even down to the detail of their clothes ;
whereupon the king blessed the name of the God of
Israel (for the second time in his career) and exempted
the three young men from participation in Babylonian
forms of worship, anything to the contrary notwithstanding. Furthermore : ' By me therefore this decree
is made, that every people, tribe, and tongue which
shall speak blasphemy against the God of Sidrach,
Misach, and Abdenago shall be destroyed and their
houses laid waste ; for there is no other God that can

---

[1] For this reference to the ' Son of God ' I presume to copy the
note which is given in Fr Hugh Pope's *Aids*, Vol. II. ' " It is hard
to understand," says St Jerome, " how this wicked king could have
deserved to see the Son of God," he therefore prefers to follow
Symmachus who read " sons of God " or the angels ' (p. 336).

save in this manner.' To crown all the Hebrew ex-ministers were reinstated. So the affair ends on a distinctly hopeful note. When Daniel comes back from his tour of the provinces there will be nothing but good news to await him. Unless . . .

iii

Unless this sort of thought suggests itself to the Prophet's mind : that the incident of the golden Dura image is a direct sequel to the Divine Revelation about the image in Nabuchodonosor's dream—which also possessed a golden crown. It looks rather as if God's favour is being turned into an insult against Himself : He reveals a hidden idea and receives for return an idol ; He loads Nabuchodonosor with riches—to see them being spent on Marduk. And how readily do men sell themselves for the gold that has come from His treasuries ! Truly have men's eyes been dazzled so that they cannot see the sun ! And if the case is such in the time of the golden head, what will it be in the day of the silver arms ? in the day of the brazen trunk ? in the day of the iron legs ? Man is commanded to worship GOD, and not for the first time in history does man write an ' l ' between the last two letters of His Name—and worship an image made with hands.

CHAPTER VI

THE KING'S SECOND DREAM
(Daniel iv, 1–24.)

i

THIS chapter opens with a royal proclamation :
Nabuchodonosor is recounting before all his
people the latest of Daniel's signal services to the crown.

> ' I, Nabuchodonosor, was at rest in my house
> and flourishing in my palace. I saw a dream that
> affrighted me . . . then I set forth a decree that all
> the wise men of Babylon should be brought in
> before me, and that they should show me the
> interpretation of the dream.'

The lamentable absence of dates makes it impossible,
as I have already suggested in connexion with the
previous episode, to fix these incidents with any degree
of accuracy. The present story seems to follow close
upon the heels of the other : Daniel's timely arrival
to ' declare the dream ' having quite probably coincided
with his return from the tour which had kept him
away from the Dedication on the plain of Dura.

The dream on this occasion has at least one advantage over its predecessor : the substance of what was
dreamt has remained in the mind of the dreamer.
But even so the fact that Nabuchodonosor had been

' seeing things again ' must have caused no small anxiety in the wise men's palace. We can imagine the comments : ' If only he would take something for it . . . these state banquets before going to bed are bound to upset a man's sleep . . . the physicians and not the magicians are the people for this particular kind of crisis ' . . . and so on.

' Then came in the wise men and the soothsayers and I told the dream before them ; but they did not show me the interpretation thereof till their colleague Daniel came in before me . . . and I told the dream before him.' It is certain, then, that the Chaldeans were consulted before the Israelite. One would have thought that if Nabuchodonosor had progressed at all in the direction of the One True God he would have turned to the Lord in his distress of mind and not to the gods who had played him false before. Perhaps he wanted to consult the Lord but was obliged, for reasons of precedence, to hear what the ministers of other gods might say ; it was, after all, a state affair and not merely a matter of the royal conscience. And perhaps (I have suggested this already) Daniel was not yet home from the provinces. In any case the text implies that Daniel had a perfect right to be present among the wise men, and was not—as on the former discussion of dreams—summoned only at his own request ; this time it looks as if Daniel was merely rather late. We are not told what the wise men had to say about the dream ; they were evidently less talkative than the group who were consulted before. And, like the chorus of Peers in *Iolanthe*, having nothing very much to say, they said it very nicely . . . and were waved out of the presence of the king to make room for the next lot. Then comes

Daniel. ' And I told the dream before him,' recounts
the king. This is it :

A great tree rises up out of the middle of the earth ;
spreading visibly it amazes the whole world with its
size, beauty and fruitfulness ; every kind of bird dwells
in its branches and every kind of beast is sheltered
in its shadow ; all flesh is nourished by its fruit. An
angel comes down from heaven and issues a command :
' Cut down the tree,' says the angel, ' and chop off the
branches thereof ; shake off its leaves and scatter its
fruits ; let the beasts fly away that are under it and
the birds from its branches ; nevertheless leave the
stump of its roots in the earth, and let it be tied with
a band of iron and of brass among the grass that is
without ; and let it be wet with the dew of heaven,
and let its portion be with the wild beasts that are in
the grass of the earth.' Here the angel seems to endow
the tree—what is left of it, that is to say the stump
—with personality, because he goes on to say : ' Let
his heart be changed from man's, and let a beast's
heart be given him ; and let seven times pass over
him . . . till the living know that the Most High ruleth
in the kingdom of men, and He will give it to whomsoever it shall please Him . . .' Such was the dream
which Daniel was asked to explain. Also he was asked
to do so at once : ' O Baltassar, tell me quickly the
interpretation . . . thou art able because the spirit
of the holy gods is in thee.' (Daniel's Chaldean name,
we must remind ourselves, was Baltassar.) It seems,
then, that Nabuchodonosor had guessed that the
dream was not one which admitted of a very encouraging explanation, and that he wished to know the worst
at once.

Now Daniel had fared well at the king's hands ; the

two men were friends. The Prophet was guiding, or trying to guide, the sovereign towards the truth. They were in sympathy on many points, and each admired the outstanding qualities of the other : Nabuchodonosor recognised sanctity in his minister, and Daniel recognised genius in his king. So the next verse is no surprise to us :

' Then Daniel began silently to think within himself for about one hour ; and his thoughts troubled him.' It is not difficult to reconstruct the scene. The Prophet is still—if we are right in supposing him to have come straight from his journey to the palace—in his travelling clothes ; the king, having received audiences all the morning, is in his royal purple. Daniel, ' thinking silently within himself,' paces up and down in the garden for a good sixty minutes. An Elias or a Jeremias would not have ' thought within himself ' for half the time. Daniel shrinks terribly from giving pain, and he knows very well that however gracefully he handles the matter of the king's dream there must inevitably be sorrow and dread ; he is in a distinctly delicate position. He decides to do the difficult thing, the only possible thing ; he has prayed about it, and he must leave the rest to God. He stands for a moment on the terrace in the sun, and then taps gently at the shutters that lead into the hall where the king is waiting. . . . It is Nabuchodonosor who speaks first.

' Let not the dream and the interpretation thereof trouble thee, O Baltassar,' says the king ; and the remark tells us much of the characters of the two men. It shows that Daniel possessed the gift of sympathy—rare in that rugged line of Hebrew prophets—to a marked degree : the anticipated sharing of his friend's sorrow was revealing itself, evidently, in his expression.

And then on Nabuchodonosor's part : ' Let it not trouble thee.' ' *Thee*,' notice, and not ' us.' What exquisite fineness of feeling the man must have had ! How much he seems to be improving on the Nabuchodonosor that we knew at first ! ' Well, anyway,' he seems to be saying, ' *you* needn't worry, my dear friend, it's not *your* fault that I've got myself into trouble . . . because I suppose it *is* trouble, judging by the expression on your face.' Then Daniel tells him what the dream is about.

' My lord, the dream be to them that hate thee, and the interpretation thereof to thy enemies.' This is the way the Prophet breaks his news, so wording the introduction as to let the gloom of its import sink in by stages. ' The tree which thou sawest which was high and strong . . . it is thou, O king, who art grown great and become mighty . . .' and then he goes on to interpret the angel's message. The ruling of God, Nabuchodonosor must know, is that ' they shall cast thee out from among men, and thy dwelling shall be with the cattle and the wild beasts ; and thou shalt eat grass like an ox, and thou shalt be wet with the dew of heaven ; and seven times shall pass over thee *till thou know that the Most High ruleth over the kingdom of men, and that He giveth it to whomsoever He will.* But ' —and here, surely, we can mark the softening of the Prophet's voice almost to a whisper—' whereas He commanded that the stumps of the roots thereof (that is of the tree) should be left, thy kingdom shall remain to thee *after thou shalt have known that power is from heaven.*'

So that was what Nabuchadonosor was given to consider. One might have thought that, with the previous dream to go upon, even the magicians would have made something of the data at their disposal. It was not a difficult dream as dreams go. Perhaps the magicians *had* been able to make something of it but were loth to reveal their deductions—masking their reluctance under a show of ignorance. True, it was not the kind of mask that had served very well in the past, but then almost anything was better than telling an irascible sovereign that he was soon to go mad.

The idea of a tree, incidentally, as signifying national prosperity is a familiar one. Not only to Jews,[1] but perhaps even more to Babylonians, the ' tree-motif ' would have been full of meaning. ' In Eridu a palm stalk grew overshadowing ; in a holy place did it become green. . . . Into the heart of its holy house, which spread its shade like a forest, hath no man entered,'—this is from an ancient Chaldean hymn of praise to the sacred tree, quoted from Miss Duff and Mr Hope's book already referred to ; these authors write in this connexion (p. 50) : ' On the walls of the mighty idol temples which Nabuchadnezzar has built in every street in Babylon is the oft-repeated picture of the sacred tree carved in stone. In some of these pictures kings and priests stand worshipping with uplifted hands. Before other tree images strange winged figures stand, offering rich gifts.' But in spite of the fact that Nabuchodonosor would have seen trees on every side of him, whether in his palace or in his gardens or in the temple, there is no earthly reason to believe that this vision of his was what psychologists now refer to as a ' dream-reflex.' If it was, then it

[1] Compare Nabuchodonosor's tree with Ezechiel's cedar (Ezechiel xxxi, 3).

was the kind of ' dream-reflex ' that Almighty God
saw fit to inspire.

ii

The king, poor man, will learn his lesson at a cost.
The truth that even a nation's fortunes—let alone a
single individual's—must come under the direction of
Divine Providence would appear, one might have
thought, fairly obvious. Yet it was precisely this that
Nabuchodonosor would not see. Deane (op. cit.,
pp. 79–80) cites Diodorus to show that the Babylonians believed very distinctly in Divine Providence ;
' they held,' writes Dr Deane, ' that nothing took place
on earth without the consent of the gods. These,
however, required to be informed of what took place
upon earth, and accordingly they had their messenger,
Papsukal, just as in Greek mythology the sun
acquainted the gods with what occurred.' But it was
no good Nabuchodonosor knowing about the ways of
Providence in theory only ; he would have to learn
the force of it by bitter experience. People like
Nabuchodonosor learn their lessons by means of practical demonstration : he needed to be swept—in body
as well as in mind—to the opposite end of the road he
was now travelling. It seems that God was so anxious
to have this soul for Himself that, other and gentler
advances having failed, He must win it by the exercise
of His Power ; He must break Nabuchodonosor and
build him up anew. This is not God's way as a rule,
but there are some souls who are so tenacious, and at
the same time so worth having, that when they have
proved themselves deaf to the Divine hint it is only
the Divine violence that can reduce them to the
speechlessness which listens, eventually, to the voice

of grace. When God goes to such lengths over a soul it means that He intends to be very much loved indeed.

Daniel, looking into the man in front of him, must have been fully alive to the potentialities of Nabuchodonosor's soul; the Prophet must have seen the heights to which the king could climb. And he certainly saw the path that was mapped out for the ascent. The proud spirit would have to go a long way down the hill before it could start mounting the other side of the valley. It would be a way of pain, a way which would seem to be taking so much out of him as to leave, apparently, not even what was essentially sound; it would be an 'unreasonable' way, and yet it would be the only way in which that warped and stubborn spirit might be straightened out and made pliable. 'Unless the grain of wheat falling to the ground dieth, itself remaineth alone. But if it die, it bringeth forth much fruit.' Was there ever a better illustration than the case of Nabuchodonosor? 'He that loveth his life,' the text goes on to say, 'shall lose it, and he that hateth his life in this world keepeth it unto life eternal.'[1]

One would like to think that Daniel was permitted to see, side by side with the great tree-trunk of which he had been talking to the king, another tree—a slender Vine this time—and that he would have longed with all his heart to reveal its beauties to the king; that he would have longed to explain the necessity of ' abiding in the Vine ' . . . of accepting all that great strength of his as coming from the Lord . . . and further, that because he, Nabuchodonosor, had borne no fruit as yet he must be ' taken away ' and be ' purged,' so that one day he might ' bring forth much fruit,' and that

[1] John xii, 24, 25.

his fruit ' should remain.' But what would have been the use of telling all this to the king ? The wisdom of Daniel was resorted to by the king only as a sort of hand-book of the unseen ; the knowledge of God which his friend possessed was used by Nabuchodonosor solely when an emergency revealed the inadequacy of his own ; the advice of his Hebrew minister was certainly more worth having than the advice of his other counsellors . . . but a course of religious instruction was, quite simply, not what the king was after. This would have to be supplied, in a different form altogether, by God Himself.

If, however, Daniel refrained from enlarging upon the theme of finding one's roots in God alone, at least he took the opportunity of pointing out the line of conduct which he thought Nabuchodonosor should adopt :

' Wherefore, O king, let this counsel be acceptable to thee, and redeem thou thy sins with alms and thy iniquities with works of mercy to the poor ; perhaps He will forgive thy offences.' The Prophet seems to be saying to himself : ' God alone can teach him, but there's no harm in showing to God that he's willing to learn.' The plain-spoken programme which Daniel puts before the king further suggests that Nabuchodonosor's world-wide advancement had been effected at a certain cost to justice. But as a matter of fact the king himself admits as much ; there is an inscription of his which reads : ' I stirred up the disobedient and I collected the poor, and I gave full directions for the work.' If not at direct oppression these words hint at the exploitation of forced labour, and when we remember the vast undertakings which Nabuchodonosor had carried through during the early part of his reign

H

(in his quite unregenerate days—when he was putting out people's eyes[1] and sentencing whole palacefuls of people to death) it is not necessarily uncharitable to surmise that his methods may have departed from the accepted standards of strict justice. But then we have very little notion of what *were* the accepted standards of justice ; Oriental despotism of the sixth century B.C. allows of a generous margin. Anyway, if the king will only turn over a new leaf, says Daniel, who knows but that God ' will forgive thy offences ' ? The Protestant version has, instead of these words, ' if it may be a lengthening of thy tranquillity,' which perhaps better expresses what we feel to have been the mind of Daniel—namely : ' Do penance and *of course* God will forgive your sins . . . and He *may* also shorten the days of your punishment.'

Thus the interview closes not entirely on a note of gloom : Daniel is reminding the king that the tree has not been *uprooted*—far from it—but severed, merely, from the trunk. ' Thy kingdom shall remain to thee after thou shalt have known that power is from heaven.' God isn't punishing you exactly : it's only that He wants this kingdom properly run ; the moment you are mentally in a position to run it properly you shall have it back again . . . but you *must* remember that power is from heaven.

The benefit that Nabuchodonosor derived from this heart-to-heart talk was, as we shall see (and as we have doubtless guessed even if we have not known it from our childhood days), negligible. Admonitions, inspirations, eye-openers, they were all lost on him. He would not bow his neck—yet—to the One True God.

[1] 4 Kings xxv, 7.

CHAPTER VII

THE FULFILMENT OF THE DREAM
(*Daniel iv*, 26–34.)

i

MOST of us fall pretty easily into a category according to whether we follow principles, people, or possessions. In the long run we are best off if we follow principles—provided they are the right ones ; people, too, are worth following—provided they are the right ones ; it is only when we follow property that our souls assume the dimensions of a lemon-pip. It is good for man to be in love because if he loves rightly it means that he will be unselfish. This is true if the object of his love be either an ideal (a cause, a policy, a hope, religion) or a person. But if he loves *things* he will want them for the pleasure he can get out of them : he worships self. Nabuchodonosor, I am afraid, loved things.

' At the end of twelve months he [Nabuchodonosor] was walking in the palace of Babylon. And the king said : Is not this the great Babylon which I have built to be the seat of the kingdom by the strength of my power and the glory of my excellence ? And while the word was yet in the king's mouth a voice came down from heaven : To thee, O king Nabuchodonosor, it is said : Thy kingdom shall pass from thee.' Yes indeed,

O foolish king, these were foolish thoughts . . . could you not have laughed them from you ?

So it took only a year for the first sign of the sentence's fulfilment to make its appearance. The penalty seems almost to be hastened by the vanity which pleads guilty to the offence. Poor Nabuchodonosor, perhaps there was provocation enough ! Look at the Babylon which meets his eyes . . .

We have seen Nabuchodonosor on his balcony before, preening himself in the morning sun and toying—but less advertently—with such ideas as these. We can fancy him up there again, or pacing the marble-paved terraces that look towards the south. As he gazes out over the city he can make a very fair estimate as to how far he himself has contributed towards Babylon's expansion. Dotted about in front of him are the onion-shaped domes of local shrines and temples, new and gleaming gold in the fierce glare of the sun. They are *his*, he has put them there. He sees the enormous arcaded arena over by the eastern gate of the city . . . it had been a particularly engaging toy of his a few years ago, for as long as the building operations had lasted. There is the famous Processional Way[1] . . . again *his* undertaking. The baths, too (which, thinks the king to himself, have done so much to keep the military out of mischief under peace-time conditions . . . some sort of club-life has had to be provided in Babylon to take the place of the drawing-room gatherings which have unfitted so many for the service of

[1] This paved thoroughfare which led from the palace of the king to the temple of Marduk exists in parts to-day. On it was the Ishtar Gate (built also by Nabuchodonosor) which resembled a fortress more than an entrance ; on the inside it was faced with enamel in low relief. Nabuchodonosor would have been able to see this inner façade from his balcony or terrace.

arms) . . . yes, he could confidently say that he had introduced the baths to Babylon. The flower-gardens ; the public parks ; the slender canals which looked like ribbons of silver thrown over the landscape by a retreating goddess ; the distant patches of green, flecked with the pin-prick white of a marble pavilion or villa, proclaiming the wealth of a Babylonian noble ; those vast sheets of water that looked like lakes, but were really reservoirs ;[1] those gigantic walls of brick and stone ; those bridges that were to baffle future historians (so rapid is the flood of the Euphrates that without the helps of modern science it would seem almost impossible that the uprights should ever have been planted in the river bed) ; and, last of all, the great image of gold that still stood up bold and defiant in the plain of Dura[2] . . . yes, all these things were *his*, his own personal playthings, and but for his stupendous initiative would never have been there. How much he enjoyed them, and how fully did he intend to hold on to them.

And so what with one thing and another—material success, beautiful surroundings, peace at home and abroad—a sense of general well-being settled upon the soul of Nabuchodonosor which a more spiritually-

[1] Water was drawn at immense expense from the Euphrates by a system of small canals ; the two reservoirs which were thereby formed provided the city with an abundant supply of water all the year round and at the same time irrigated the hanging-gardens. A canal was eventually constructed which linked up the Tigris with the Euphrates.

[2] Though the Dedication was probably not one of the days to which the king looked back with the most pleasure, there is no hint in the pages of history, sacred or profane, that the image on Dura was taken down. Nabuchodonosor, though he was prepared to admit the claims—some of them—of the One True God, was not prepared—*yet*, at all events—to remove an idol which he approved of æsthetically. The thing was an elegant decoration if nothing else, and would therefore have to stay.

minded man would have had reason to suspect. How dangerous is satisfaction, how treacherous the glow which comes of triumph ! ' Not unto us, O Lord, not unto us ; but unto Thy name give glory.'[1] The roll of drums which accompanies success prevents us from hearing this protestation of the Psalmist. Success makes men love the world too well ; it stills in man the ' expectation that waiteth for the revelation of the sons of God.'[2] There is always a hope for us when we ' groan and are in labour,' because the chances are that we shall be sensible enough to ' look to the glory that is to come, that shall be revealed,' but with satisfaction comes a halting in the way, a willingness to forgo ' what the eye hath not seen nor the ear heard.' A *contented* soul (in the sense of one who has ' got there ' in this world and who is enjoying himself all he can) no longer tries ' to comprehend with all the saints what is the breadth and length and height and depth.'[3] God forbid that we should ever rest content !

Nabuchodonosor committed, not for the first time but for the first time in this *way*, the sin of idolatry. He worshipped the intermediate. He put the things of this world first, and, having gained as many of them as he wanted, he, quite logically, gave up wanting. But man *must* want. He must even want something which he knows he cannot get—here. If he limits his desires to those which, given a certain amount of luck and careful management, he can satisfy, there is the awful possibility that his goal may one day be reached—and that he rest content. ' Brethren, I do not count myself to have apprehended ; but one thing I do ; forgetting the things that are behind and

[1] Psalm cxiii, 1.   [2] Romans viii, 19.
[3] Ephesians iii, 18.

stretching forth myself to those that are before, I press towards the mark, to the prize of the supernal vocation of God in Christ Jesus Our Lord.'[1] The serenity of the saints is not due to the fact that they have ceased to ' press towards the mark ' (that they have *arrived* at what they were aiming at), nor is it a reward, primarily, for their having ' pressed ' so generously ; it is rather a serenity that comes of a certainty : the certainty of what they are after . . . and of Him ' Who is faithful Who will do it.'[2] It is a ' supernal vocation ' that we are created to follow, and the Voice will be fulfilled in Its good time. Daniel and Nabuchodonosor were both ' men of desires ' : the difference being that with Daniel the desires amounted to the theological virtue of Hope, with Nabuchodonosor they ended up in the vice which the textbooks call covetousness. The Prophet went *on*, the king stopped.

Nabuchodonosor might almost have been mentioned by name when Our Lord was speaking of the ' certain rich man ' to whom the Father said : ' Thou fool, this night do they require thy soul of thee.'[3] The rich man rested in his peace when he should have known that ' requiescat in pace ' is a prayer that a man must wait for until he die. There are two kinds of peace, and the ' peace which the world giveth '[4] is a fearful thing ; it makes us accept the world that gives it. To meet the world on its own level, to accept the world in terms of time and not of eternity, *that* is the pagan thing, *that* is the attitude of the contented worldling. St Paul tells us that we must ' use this world as though we used it not '[5] . . . St James that our life is ' a vapour

---

[1] Philippians iii, 13, 14. [2] 1 Thessalonians v, 24.
[3] Luke xii, 16, 17. [4] John xiv, 27.
[5] 1 Cor. vii, 31.

which appeareth for a little while and afterwards shall vanish away.'[1] We forget these things.

Must we then, like the saints, fly to the deserts and spurn the things which God has made so good ? No, God's creatures may be—must be—loved ; but they must be loved carefully. There is a condition to be observed : creatures must not take the place of the Creator ; we may have no other gods beside Him. But ' things ' are good, ' people ' are good ; God saw that they were good—very good. It is only that our approach to them has been coloured by the sin of Adam. We can love good things wrong. We can see them out of perspective . . . and love them so—out of their order. This is surely what St Thomas has in mind when he says that all sin is the grasping of the means instead of the end. When we sin we choose to rest in a creature ; and creatures are intended to be stepping-stones to God. God's earthly creation is taken for sole satisfaction ; creatures are no longer loved as *His*, but as ours. Creatures are as it were the utterance of God, His expression *ad extra*, and it is not for us to separate the Speaker from His voice. God is One.

But the saints, we cry, what of them ? Have not the saints fled from the love of creatures ? To which it must be answered that the saints knew as well as anybody (and much better, of course) that, unless there happened to be a conflict between the two loves, the love of the creature in no way necessitated the lessening of the love of God . . . *but* that creatures must be loved in their right place. The sunshine must be loved *as* sunshine—and not as everlasting light. The reason why the saints have done their best to cut themselves

[1] James iv, 15.

off from sunshine is because they wanted to keep their sight for the vision of the Sun of Justice Itself. The saints were afraid of being blinded by the reflected light in the puddle. The saints have taught us to use creatures *as* creatures : toys which are lent to us for a time and which have to be laid down when God sees fit to give us something better to do than merely to play on the nursery floor. This does not detract from the value or dignity of God's creation, it merely means that until we see God in creatures and creatures in God we must walk very warily indeed . . . stepping lightly over the world's surface on our way to Him. ' A man's life doth not consist in the abundance of the things which he possesseth,'[1] but we can remember for our consolation at the same time that ' there is nothing from without a man that, entering into him, can defile him ; but the things which come from a man, those are they that defile a man.'[2] And the same is found in St Paul who cries out with a glorious confidence that ' neither things present nor things to come, nor might, nor height, nor depth, *nor any other creature* shall be able to separate us from the love of God.'[3]

On the other hand quite a number of creatures, alas, were allowed by Nabuchodonosor to get in between his soul and God.

ii

Let us particularise all this by examining the very case of Nabuchodonosor.

He looks about him and revels in it all ; and not having the supernatural in view he reads all wrong what he revels in. His approach is that of the ' carnal

---

[1] Luke xii, 15.   [2] Mark vii, 15.
[3] Romans viii, 38, 39.

man.' The materialist eye is veiled: he has looked so long at creatures that he cannot see their meaning.[1]

[1] Fr Martindale, commenting on Romans i, 20–32 (which contains the passage ' for the invisible things of Him are clearly seen, being understood by the things that are made . . . so that they are inexcusable, because that when they knew God they have not glorified Him as God nor given thanks, but became vain in their thoughts, and their foolish heart was darkened . . . who changed the truth of God into a lie, and worshipped and served the creature rather than the Creator. . . . *And as they liked not to have God in their knowledge, God delivered them up to a reprobate sense*'), says as follows:

' Paul's charge is that, having a *true* knowledge of God . . . men acted against it. Forthwith the evil choice begins to blind them, human ignorance is, at least where it involves positive error, the result of sin; and each new sin drives the sinner's mind deeper into its guilty ignorance. (Footnote: Commentators here rightly quote four famous passages—from Aristotle, who says that the Invisible is seen from [his] very works; from Philo, that from [his] works we ascend, as by some heavenly ladder, to surmise, by a probable argument, the Artificer; the Book of Wisdom, affirming that from the greatness and beauty of creatures men can analogously contemplate their Originator; and the decision of the Vatican Council, that men can, from creatures, ascend to a sure knowledge of the Creator. It is striking how each author speaks accurately from his own standpoint. Aristotle, the Greek deductive philosopher, regards creatures as premises from which the existence of the First Cause may be argued; the half-Platonized Philo regards them mystically as a ladder by which one may rise to the place of mystical intuition; the Book of Wisdom, though nearer to the thought of Alexandria, is exactly right when it says we can get a true though analogical knowledge of God through creatures; and St Paul speaks like a true Jew when he thinks in terms of God's power rather than of His causality—a Greek concept Paul sees creatures as a mirror of God.) If you read carefully St Paul's frightful list of sins that he lays to the charge of the pagan, you detect at first sight a sort of diminuendo; after the great crimes you come to dullness . . . hardness. . . . But as you carefully study the records of Greece and Rome you seem to find, along with increased refinement, with complication of mind, with a sensitivity augmented to the point of neurasthenia, a parallel lessening of gentleness, tenderness, human insight, depth of mind and feeling. . . . This *thinness of mind and of feeling*, this real lack of something human which could and should be there, *does indeed seem to us noticeable in those who have lost the habit and power of associating with spiritual things.* In order adequately to live in your congenital three dimensions you must have been admitted to, made at home in, a fourth.' (*Princes of His People : St Paul*, pp. 157–8.) The italics are mine.

He sees only the outside of things, their shapes and colours ; and he is perfectly prepared to take this second-best interpretation ; he asks no more of life than what the ' concupiscence of the eyes ' can give him. Yes, he marvels at the Wonders of Nature, but he marvels at all the wrong things about it. Well, he must be taught—out of doors and right up against nature in the raw—how to look upon creation with a purer eye. That giant intellect which has planned cities and guided kingdoms will be reduced to the poverty of a beast's—it will be without reason ; the pasture-land, which he has substituted for the desert waste that was there before, will provide him with grass —to munch ; the skies, which he has regarded as a good enough canopy to go over his crowned head, will pour down rain upon his shoulders—shoulders that have borne the purple ; the sun, which he has even wor-shipped for a time, will expose the filth of his condition in the broad light of day ; the very game that he and his nobles have stalked—the boar, the deer, the buffalo —will amuse themselves by stalking *him* . . . him, Nabuchodonosor, clambering over the rocks on all fours and covered in mud and slime. A dictator come to be an indifferently skilful beast, an object not respected by the lowest living thing.

' All these things came upon Nabuchodonosor . . . he was driven away from among men and did eat grass like an ox, and his body was wet with the dew of heaven ; till his hair grew like the feathers of eagles and his nails like birds' claws.' No detail of the pro-gramme was left out. He had been accused, and out of his own mouth he had condemned himself : ' the strength of my power . . . the glory of my excellence.' He had believed in the supernatural but only as a possible safeguard to the natural. The due order of things must be obeyed.

' Now at the end of the days,' continues the proclamation which we quoted at the beginning of this chapter, ' I, Nabuchodonosor, lifted up my eyes to heaven and my sense was restored to me. And I blessed the most High, and I praised and glorified Him that liveth for ever and ever ; *for His Power is an everlasting Power, and His Kingdom is to all generations.*'

So there is no mistaking the fact that Nabuchodonosor learned his lesson.

First of all, how long did his madness last ? The angel had said that ' seven times ' would have to pass over him before he should be cured ; the words ' at the end of days ' suggest that the period was not shortened. Opinion appears to be richly divided as to the length of time signified by ' seven times.' Some say weeks, some say months, and Josephus (who wherever possible inclines to the gloomier view) assures us that no less than seven years was the duration of the trial ; Theodoret halves the time. Miss Duff and Mr Hope do not pronounce.[1] Nor, therefore, dare I. But as a matter of fact neither the time it lasted nor the precise nature of the disease needs attention here (Pusey discusses both points fully, and somewhat pedantically, in his justly famous *Lectures on Daniel the Prophet*) ; suffice us to know that the man was intellectually pinioned, that his condition was such that he had to be driven away from people, and that the whole thing lasted long enough for his hair and finger-nails to get into a horrible state.

[1] Nor do Deane and Driver ; in fact most of the moderns leave the matter (wisely) in mid-air.

Listen to what he goes on to say in his proclamation :
' All the inhabitants of the earth are reputed as nothing
before Him, for He doth according to His will . . . as
well with the powers of heaven as among the inhabitants
of the earth ; and there is none that can resist His hand
and say to Him : Why hast Thou done it ? ' Such is
the confession of the *revenant ;* and can anything be
fairer than that last phrase ? ' We've no right whatever,' says the newly enlightened king, ' to question
the decisions of Providence—even if they seem to
produce chaos at the time.' Nabuchodonosor rises
from his humiliation a noble being. Only the finest
natures are the stronger for degradation. The grain
of wheat has died and grown again. The phœnix has
risen from the ashes.

' I lifted up my eyes to heaven.' Yes, and I saw a
new heaven and a new earth . . . because I saw for the
first time Whom it was Who had made them—and why
. . . so that it was not *until* I ' raised my eyes to
heaven '—wrenching away my gaze from self and things
—that I was able to ' praise and glorify Him that liveth
for ever.' Like a spring released, the mind of Nabuchodonosor has leapt free ; free, not so much from the
darkness of his madness as from the false light of his
previous sanity. He can speak now of the Lord's everlasting Power and of the nothingness of man ; of the
folly of resistance and of the arrogance of doubting
His decrees. He tastes the freshness of life as a man
might taste the freshness of the open country after
walking through a tunnel from his suburb. The same
is the dawn of contemplative prayer after years in the
night of the senses : all of what was seen before is seen
again, but seen now in a different perspective—seen
in its relation to its Author. Creation is recognised

as being made up of the same entities that were enjoyed in the light before the darkness, but it is recognised now in its true terms ; people and things are loved now, not because they are familiar and reminiscent of a previous happiness, but because their place in the plan is understood—they are loved for what they are and not for what they bring. The universe is edged with gold, and all creation sings the praises of the Lord.

Nabuchodonosor must have felt, when once he had come through his crisis, as a man would feel who has for years taken a box at the Opera and the Ballet but who, sitting with his back to the stage, has contented himself with looking at Medici reproductions of Renoir and Degas ; not that singing or acting or dancing are more important than painting (I don't think they are ; in fact I think they are nothing like *as* important) but that one is the shadow merely—the re-presentation —of the other. Creatures are the shadow (or, to use St Thomas's expression, the 'footprint') of the Creator. When I say that Nabuchodonosor felt like the theatre-goer who woke up to his mistake (and who in future, doubtless, turned his chair round the other way) I mean that he felt a fool. Which was about the best thing in the world he could have felt : the 'foolishness of men' is the best possible preparation for the 'wisdom' which is of God).[1]

---

[1] It may be of interest to notice how exactly the Psalmist voices the sentiments and experience attributed to Nabuchodonosor in the foregoing pages ; freedom from the captivity of the senses makes David (or if not David, the writer to whom the credit is given) sing the prayers which Nabuchodonosor is to echo. ' Our soul hath passed through a torrent . . . and hath been delivered as a sparrow out of the snare . . . the snare is broken and we are delivered ' (cxxiii). ' When the Lord brought back the captivity we became like men comforted ; then was our mouth filled with gladness and

iii

The return of Lazarus to the little world of Bethany
can hardly have been more touching than Nabuchodonosor's re-entry into the great world of Babylon.
Reading between the lines, Nabuchodonosor must,
despite the unpleasant tendencies which we have seen
him yielding to during the earlier part of his reign, have
been a lovable man in many ways ; and the majority
of his courtiers seem also to have had their good points.
See how Nabuchodonosor's proclamation continues :

> ' My sense returned to me, and I came to the
> honour and glory of my kingdom ; and my shape
> returned to me ; and my nobles and my magis-
> trates sought for me ; and I was restored to my
> kingdom ; and greater majesty was added to me.'

our tongue with joy . . . the Lord hath done great things for us
and we are become joyful . . . they that sow in tears shall reap
in joy ' (cxxv). What did Nabuchodonosor learn if not the
Psalmist's constant doctrine that ' unless the Lord build the house
they labour in vain that build it ' (cxxvi) ? Quite truly could the
king have said on the day that his wits were cleared : ' Thou hast
put away my acquaintance far from me, they have set me an
abomination to themselves ; I was delivered up . . . my eyes
languished through poverty . . . but I, O Lord, have cried to Thee,
and in the morning my prayer shall prevent Thee . . . O Lord
God of Hosts, who is like to Thee ? . . . Thou rulest the power of
the sea . . . *Thou hast humbled the proud one* . . . *Thine* are the
heavens and *Thine* is the earth ; the world and the fulness thereof
Thou hast founded . . . blessed is the people that knoweth jubila-
tion, they shall walk in the light of Thy countenance and in Thy
name they shall rejoice all the day, and in Thy justice they shall be
exalted, *for Thou art the glory of their strength*, and in *Thy* good
pleasure shall our horn be exalted. For our protection is of the
Lord and of our King, the Holy One of Israel . . . in the morning
shall man grow up like grass, in the morning shall he flourish and
pass away . . . *we have rejoiced for the days in which Thou hast
humbled us*, for the years in which we have seen evil . . . let the
brightness of the Lord be upon us, and *direct Thou the work of
our hands over us ;* yea, the work of our hands do Thou direct '
(lxxxvii, lxxxviii, lxxxix).

The picture is delightful : a humble monarch is being led from the paddock which has been his resting-place during all those long ' seven times ' ; he is being led gently, as if he were some infinitely precious scarecrow, by gorgeously dressed nobles and civic dignitaries. If the central figure of the party is shy in spite of his happiness, those who cluster round are shy also . . . pretending not to notice their master's hair, beard, and finger-nails. The ministers are in a doubt as to how much of ceremony is due to their friend as king, and how much love may fittingly be shown to him as man. We like to think of the solemn little procession winding in and out between the flower-beds and up the terraces towards the palace . . . gardeners open-mouthed and holding their hats in their hands. Silence is still observed as the king is bowed into one of the ground-floor rooms, and then, out of sight from the eyes of the curious, the party breaks into friendly disorder. . . .

We cannot picture this scene without making Nabuchodonosor into a perfectly charming person—which I honestly think is what he was ! We see him here as a smiling and blinking figure, grateful for the confidence of his friends and still more grateful for the blessings of the Lord. While the courtiers are pressing round him and protesting (incredibly) that they never doubted his return, the various masters of the royal suite are busy about their several offices. The robes of state are being laid out, the bath is being prepared, the royal bedchamber is being aired and got ready, and all along the line of windows that mark the king's private suite there is the business of opening shutters that have got stuck with long disuse. (A thoughtful observer might have seen something symbolical in this last detail of the king's return.)

While upstairs the palace is alive with the swift movement and shrill whispers of barbers, perfumers, chiropodists, liveried messengers, and excited ministers, below—in the royal kitchens—the scene is every bit as animated : cooks, cheered at the opportunity which is offered by the occasion, hurry to exact the utmost of their art.

.   .   .   .   .

A holiday is proclaimed in Babylon.

The squares and market-places are filled with every kind and condition of man. The air of festivity is all the more keen because the whole thing has been such a surprise. Everywhere the conversation comes back to the one topic. Nobody can talk about anything else. Special prayers of thanksgiving have been offered up in all the temples of the city. Lengthy votes of confidence are being read out at half a dozen municipal assemblies. But—and I hope we can carry conjecture thus far—there is never a hint dropped at any of these public functions (or a joke made, or a question asked, or a fear expressed) about what went on, during the 'seven times,' in the fields and woods from which the people of Babylon have been so rigorously excluded. The past is closed for ever—like the little grass paddock itself. The king alone, in his new-found meekness, may refer to the time of his pain.

.   .   .   .   .

There is a verse from the seventy-second Psalm to which one would like to think that Daniel drew the king's attention. 'I was become as a beast before Thee,' is the humble prayer, 'and am with Thee always ; Thou hast held me by Thy right hand, and

I

by Thy will Thou hast drawn me on, and by Thy glory
Thou hast received me. For what have I in heaven,
and what do I desire upon earth besides Thee ? '

It is interesting to hear Nabuchodonosor saying that
' *greater* majesty was added ' to him when he assumed
the crown the second time. To him certainly the words
of the Gospel applied : he received his ' hundredfold
now in this world ' as well as the promise of happiness
in the next. The angel had said that the stump of the
tree should remain and grow again ; and so indeed it
proved in the event. Outwardly Nabuchodonosor
never made the Great Renunciation (which a novelist
might have made him make) ; he made the Great
Acquiescence instead. Which was probably—in fact
must have been—of far more value in the eyes of God.

iv

We need not really dwell any further upon the story
of Nabuchodonosor ; ' and the king lived happily
ever after ' would be a perfectly adequate rounding off
to the account. It is of merely historical interest,
however (or psychological, or economical, or academical
interest—whichever you like to call it) to find that
when he returned to normal life again he found his
kingdom waiting for him and running smoothly ; it
says a lot for the good order in which he had left his
affairs, and also for the loyalty of those in whose hands
he had left them. For more than a quarter of a century
everything had been subject to his personal supervision.
The State, the Church, philosophy, art, science had
alike received their character from Nabuchodonosor ;
so that, had he not been a recognised genius, it is
inconceivable that the empire should have maintained

itself without confusion in some department or other. It is probable that Daniel (as Lord Chancellor, oracle, and friend possessing inside knowledge of the patient's case) did much during the ' seven times ' to prevent a panic—assuring the nation that the failure of the king's mind was but a temporary lapse. At all events a complete restoration to dignity and national confidence was, as we have seen, effected. But—and I think this is important—none was left in doubt as to the difference that existed between the new and the old Nabuchodonosor. One of the king's first official acts was to issue to all the world the proclamation from which we have been quoting ; he wanted everyone to know what had happened—and why. From now on, as is fitting after such an experience, we hear no more of Nabuchodonosor. Of his forty-three years of kingship it is estimated by the commentators that the last ten were years of peace. (And, one would suggest, of comparative hiddenness.) Both Deane and Pusey paint pleasing pictures of Nabuchodonosor's closing phase. We are encouraged by these writers to see (as indeed our own inclination would lead us to see) a hard-bitten hero of many conquests, the genius of Babylon's renaissance, sitting at his papers or his prayers with a grasp, at last, of the meaning of success. To have attained to that knowledge is not the least of his achievements. Success, real success, is impossible to gauge with finite faculties. We, with our little slide-rules in our hands, see one single aspect only of success—and that the least vital. We see the outward catching of the outward opportunity ; true development is measured by God alone.

And so it is that Nabuchodonosor can calmly sit and work and watch . . . not anxious any longer as to whether or not his capabilities might further be exploited. He is content to wait until the time when success and failure are revealed to him in their true terms. Nabuchodonosor has found his category : not things or people, but ideals. ' *First* the Kingdom of God, and all these things shall be added.'[1]

[1] Luke xii, 31.

CHAPTER VIII

DANIEL AND BALTASSAR
(Daniel v.)

i

FOLLOWING the events of the Prophet's career as they are given to us in the Book of Daniel it is the feast of Baltassar, to which the man of God was summoned as the party was breaking up, that next engages our attention.

> ' Baltassar the king made a great feast for a thousand of his nobles, and everyone drank according to his age.'

This was one of the most eventful evenings in the history of Babylon (as well as in that of the Prophet), so it will have to be dealt with in some detail, but before we examine the rush of dramatic incident it will be necessary to account for the very wide gap that is left between this and the incidents recorded in the previous chapter. From Scripture itself we have little enough to go upon in our effort to reconstruct the intervening history ; Jeremias and the writer of the Fourth Book of Kings are our only authorities as regards Biblical sources, and these, of course, touch upon Babylonian affairs only in so far as they are reflected in the vexed fortunes of Israel. Isaias, it is true, tells us what *will* happen—and in the event, as we shall see, it *did* happen—but since he died a century or so before our period opens he can scarcely be cited as a chronicler of the time. We have to rely, therefore, upon extra-Scriptural authority. And when we turn up the historical data we find such a wealth of material —most of which is hopelessly conflicting—that it is by no means easy to decide which of the experts (among those who have sifted the evidence and gone into the matter far more deeply than I am fitted to do) we should follow. Of the ancients, Josephus, Berosus, and Herodotus are the main witnesses—together with sundry inscriptions that are to be seen in the British Museum. From among the moderns I venture to select Fr Hugh Pope for my guide ; his conclusions tally for the most with those of Driver, while he differs from Deane, Duff and Hope, Kelly and one or two others. But, as a matter of fact, the divergence that exists between the deductions of the moderns amounts to nothing very much : relationships, dates, and the sequence of reigns are about the only fields of specula-tion. It is among the ancients that you will find all the trouble. The discrepancies between Josephus's record and the account given by the Greek historians are, I am told (though with how much truth I am not in a position to know), distinctly puzzling.

Of one fact we are certain : Nabuchodonosor died in 561 B.C. He was succeeded on the throne by his son (?) Evil-Merodach. It is of this king that we learn (from 4 Kings already mentioned) that ' in the first year of his reign he lifted up the head of Joakin king of Juda out of prison.' The same authority goes on to say that the Babylonian ' spoke kindly to him [Joakin] and set his throne above the thrones that were with him in Babylon ; and he changed his garments which he had in prison, and he ate bread always before him, all the days of his life. And he appointed him a continual allowance which was also given by him, the king, day by day all the days of his life.' Joakin was the last but one of Juda's kings. He had not been a success in Jerusalem, and after a reign of three months (during which he ' did evil before the Lord according to all that his father had done ') had surrendered to Nabuchodonosor with his family and most of his nobles.[1] Thus at the age of eighteen (which was the age at which he had followed his father, Joakim, upon the throne) Joakin was brought in chains to Babylon as Nabuchodonosor's prisoner. This was in 597 B.C., and Daniel, who had now been an exile of nine years' standing, must have had the mortification of seeing the arrival in Babylon of the man who should have been representing the best that Israel could produce. For the rest of Nabuchodonosor's reign—and there were thirty-six more years to run—Joakin seems to have been subjected to the strictest confinement. By the time he was released he had spent just twice as long in prison as he had done outside it ; one wonders how he responded to the kindly treatment of Nabuchodonosor's successor ; he was probably a little suspicious, I fancy, at first. It is odd that Daniel does not mention the presence in Babylon of his country's dethroned king ; perhaps even Nabuchodonosor's ministers were kept away from Nabuchodonosor's prey : a sombre example of the right hand not being allowed to see what the left hand had chosen to do. History does not tell us when Joakin died ; he was only fifty-four when Evil-Merodach brought him out of prison, so he may have witnessed quite a number of successions to the

[1] 4 Kings xxiv, 6–16.

Babylonian throne—as the Babylonians had witnessed quite a number of successions upon his. I am sorely tempted to reconstruct the scene of Joakin's coming forth from the palace dungeons . . . but I really feel I must leave some of these things to the imagination. Especially as I have, in this instance, absolutely no historical evidence to draw from. But the idea of two Hebrew exiles, both of noble birth, exchanging in late middle age their memories of the Jerusalem of forty years ago is, to say the least, an alluring one. Anyway it is gratifying to look at what we have got in the way of evidence, even if we allow ourselves to make no concessions whatever to the demands of fancy: Evil-Merodach was a gentle creature and treated the ex-king royally. He gave him a throne, he saw to his clothes and meals, and he gave him an annuity which was to last for the rest of his, Joakin's, life. His own, Evil-Merodach's, life came to an end three years after this, in 559, when he was succeeded by Neriglissar.

Neriglissar is spoken of by Jeremias, but by some accident (probably on the part of a copyist and not on the part of Baruch to whom the Prophet dictated most of his Prophecy) the name has been divided, and the Babylonian becomes ' Neregel, Sereser,' which, coming as it does in a list of other names, is apt to cause confusion in the mind of the searcher after accuracy. Little is known of this king beyond the fact that his three years of rule included building alterations: he continued the tradition of Nabuchodonosor. Berosus states that Neriglissar was his predecessor's brother-in-law, and that he seized the throne by violence. Berosus also says, or at all events implies, that Evil-Merodach's ' lawless and dissolute reign ' made Neriglissar's accession acceptable to the people. The reign was a short one as I have said, and Neriglissar was followed on the throne by his son, Labashi-Marduk, who, as Dr Deane quotes from Berosus, ' on account of the evil qualities he displayed was beaten to death after nine months by his friends.'

The people who beat Labashi-Marduk to death—his ' friends,' that is to say—were evidently powerful in the realm : they appointed their own nominee and crowned him. This was in 555 B.C., and the name of the new king was Nabonidus. About Nabonidus there will be a certain amount to say because, for one thing, he reigned seventeen years—longer than any of his predecessors since Nabuchodonosor—and also because a great deal of material has come down to us from his reign. Anyone walking even casually into the Babylonian Room of the British Museum cannot but be struck by the many labels which bear the name of Nabonidus.

Commentators seem to be agreed that Nabonidus was not related to his predecessor, Labashi-Marduk ; he must, however, have been in some way connected with Nabuchodonosor because when his son comes into the story we shall hear him referring to Nabuchodonosor as his ' father '—meaning, presumably, at least a grandfather on his mother's side (and at most a grandfather on his father's).[1] Nabonidus is not referred to in the Book of Daniel. From the inscriptions and the earliest historians the following are the main facts that need be noted about Nabonidus : He was a native

[1] Deane does not hesitate to call Baltassar the son of Nabonidus (p. xxviii). Pope (p. 362) quotes St Jerome as calling him the son of Labashi-Marduk, ' whom he followed.' Thus St Jerome omits Nabonidus altogether. Perhaps St Jerome (with a good many later commentators) identifies Baltassar with Nabonidus. This would have the advantage of explaining the fact that Baltassar gave his dinner *as king* when his father was still upon the throne.

of Babylon and a professing worshipper of Marduk
(the god whom Nabuchodonosor had so signally
favoured fifty years before) ; he was so far involved
in building and archæology that the affairs of state
and war were neglected during the greater part of his
reign ; this alienated the sympathies of his people ;
he then—if our conjectures are correct—appointed his
son, Baltassar, as coadjutor to manage the kingdom
for him in his frequent absences from the capital ;
it was during one of these expeditions (when he was in
all probability digging up bones at Larsa, Ur, Uruk,
or Sippar) that the incident took place which we are
about to examine in this chapter.

Before we leave the learned and not very public-
spirited king to his manuscripts and his monuments,
it is worth while noticing that though he himself had
no great love for office Nabonidus encouraged the spirit
of just authority (and with what little success we shall
see in a moment) in his son, while he deplored in
equally strong terms the utter futility of his predecessor.
Berosus (quoted by Deane) tells us how Nabonidus
referred to Labashi-Marduk as ' one who knew not
how to rule ' and who had ' placed himself on the
throne against the will of the gods.' Nabonidus held
the reins of power—albeit loosely enough—until Cyrus's
conquest of Babylon in 538 B.C. It is uncertain how
long Baltassar had been acting on his father's behalf
by the time that he yielded the city to the Persians ;
ten years before the end we read of his presiding in his
father's place, but this may be only in his capacity as
heir apparent.[1] Certain it is that Baltassar and not

---

[1] In 548 B.C. Nabonidus caused much trouble by being away at
his country palace of Teva on the occasion of a procession which was
due to take place in honour of Bel and Nebo. Baltassar was away
at the same time, and the procession fell through.

Nabonidus was the name that stood for royal power in the year 539–538—the time, that is, immediately preceding the Persian advance and final attack. At long last we can pick up again the Scripture text. What the Prophet Daniel has been doing in the way of public service to the state during these twenty-three years since Nabuchodonosor's death there is no means of knowing ; he himself says nothing about it at all ; we shall consider the question of his silence on a later page.

ii

As already quoted ' Baltassar made a great feast for a thousand of his nobles, and everyone drank according to his age.' And Baltassar, wretched man, got exceedingly drunk. It seems that he overstepped the measure accorded by custom and constitution to his age. The circumstances which led up to this banquet are worth considering (even if it necessitates the dragging in of a little more history).

The place, first of all, where the party occurred. Baltassar was occupied, during most of his regency as far as one can see, at a garrison slightly north of Babylon called Arkad or Akkad. It is believed that by the time of his recognition as king, or co-equal king with Nabonidus, he had built himself a palace at Arkad, and was there entertaining generously—with but half an eye to the dangers that threatened the realm. We ask immediately—What dangers ? Have we not witnessed the triumph of Babylon's wide-flung Empire ? Was not the prosperity of Chaldea harped upon *ad nauseam* in the chapter we have just been reading ? Yes, but all that was twenty years ago. Babylon's best period closed with the death of Nabuchodonosor ; with Evil-Merodach the rot had begun to set in. **By**

now, 538 B.C., there was only a very thin veneer of
magnificence left ; the spirit of the nation was wasted.
What dangers ? The chief external menace was that
which threatened from Persia.

If we leave Babylon and Arkad for a moment and
look at Persia, we find that Cyrus, who is the next big
figure in history after Nabuchodonosor, has fired his
people with that enthusiasm for aggrandisement which
ends either in conquest or in utter, humiliating, and
almost always permanent defeat. Right back in
600 B.C. or so—when Nabuchodonosor's ' dream-
obsessions ' were at their height—the far-sighted
leader of Babylon had not been slow to recognise in
Persia the ' kingdom of silver ' which Daniel had told
him was to supersede his own. The Persian was to be
of inferior quality to the Chaldean ; but this was so,
in the event, as regards the empire's organisation only,
not its boundaries. The sway that Cyrus ultimately
exercised exceeded geographically anything that
Chaldea, or Assyria before her, had managed to effect.
If you look at Sir George Adam Smith's *Historical
Atlas of the Holy Land* you will see, under *Empires of
the Ancient World*, the extent of Persian colonisation
in 525 B.C. This map would have staggered even the
far-sighted Nabuchodonosor (especially if he compared
it with the two maps immediately above—the Egyptian
Empire, 1450 B.C., and the Babylonian Empire, 560
B.C.). But even if the Persian conquests took some time
to reach the stage signified by the pale green in the
map, it was sufficiently widespread within half a
century of Nabuchodonosor's death to verify the
explanation of the dream.[1] Shortly before the events

[1] For further evidence of Persia's growth, and for an account of
its presiding genius, Cyrus, see Dr Lods's recent work, *The Prophets
and the Rise of Judaism, passim.*

described in Daniel's fifth chapter—the events, namely, which we are about to investigate—Cyrus had overcome Lydia, of which Sardis was the capital, and had removed Croesus (the king) in chains from the fallen city. News of this Persian triumph awoke in Babylon the fear of invasion and measures were immediately taken to secure the city against hostile approach. So wherever Baltassar had been enjoying himself before, it was certainly necessary for him to be on duty north of Babylon now—waiting the return of Cyrus's Lydian army through Mesopotamia and into Persia proper.

Thus, as we seat the guests at Baltassar's tables, we have this much information to go upon : Cyrus is near enough to Babylonian territory to cause acute anxiety, though up till now there has been no fighting ; Baltassar, doing duty for the last of a line of lethargic kings, is faced with drawing up a policy of national defence ; at home, among the Chaldeans themselves, things are every bit as bad as they seem to be abroad— treason and intrigue have been responsible for the swift succession of kings, and the loyalty of the masses has been thoroughly shaken. Now we can begin the meal.

'And being drunk,' Daniel records (going straight on from the announcement about the thousand nobles who were invited to the feast), 'he [Baltassar] commanded that they should bring the vessels of gold and silver which Nabuchodonosor his father[1] had brought away out of the temple that was in Jerusalem, that the king[2] and his nobles and his wives and his concubines might drink in them.'

[1] ' According to Hebrew usage the word " father " could be used in the sense of grandfather, or of great-grandfather, or of great-great-grandfather. . . .' Charles, *Commentary on Daniel*, p. 116.

[2] I shall adopt the Bible terminology and call the Regent what Daniel calls him—king.

Notice how Daniel plans this fifth chapter : in some ways the most dramatic and carefully constructed chapter in the whole Book. He does not open his account with a description of what went on at the assembly which preceded the banquet, the assembly to which the nobles were summoned to discuss the tense situation on the border ; the writer starts straight away with what went on at the feast. The implication seems to be that where Baltassar was concerned (a dissolute man and quite unused to war) it was always the banquet that must be the first consideration, the business of the realm coming second.[1] Daniel seems to have had small respect for the leaders of Babylon at this period, and with the Baltassar story one feels already that he has decided to let himself go. Quite clearly the Prophet enjoyed telling of Baltassar's debauch ; he has taken great care that the account should reach the public in a nicely rounded literary form. Surely the abrupt introduction is all part of this ; it gives the key to the rest. Had the curtain risen on the council-hall, the *great* scene of the drama—the *dénouement* of which his own, Daniel's speech, was to be the climax—would have required a complete re-setting. He would have had to bring us away from charts and figures and details about equipment, and make us take our places afresh amid knives and forks and wines and fruits. Daniel has a fine stage-sense. He is also acutely conscious of head-line values. ' The king made a feast for a thousand of his nobles'—forgive me for quoting it a third time—' and everyone drank according to his age.' There is a ring about it. It is . a poster.

[1] The preliminary meeting to discuss matters does not come into Daniel's narrative ; that is why I have not delayed upon it.

When the carousal was at its height, then, Baltassar commanded that the vessels which had been looted from Jerusalem in Nabuchodonosor's time should be brought to him. . . . Perhaps it is not fanciful to see in this order more than the mere wilful whim of a drunken prince. In the excitement of having, earlier on in that eventful day, addressed a ' difficult ' assembly, Baltassar probably drank more at dinner than he would normally have done ; again—and this might surely be considered incentive enough—his fears about the Persian invasion would have invited the forgetfulness which wine affords. But over and above these very ' natural ' reasons for Baltassar's getting drunk, I think we can find—when we look at what he did when he *was* drunk—another reason altogether. Is it not likely that this evening's particularly hard drinking was an attempt to drown the voice of God ? Let me explain myself.

We can recall the repeated invitations of grace which were extended to the soul of ' his father Nabuchodonosor ' ; God seems to have required something rather above the average from Baltassar as well. Now a man who has consistently run away from grace would be quite likely to want to drink himself into open defiance. Suppose God is wanting the same act of faith that was finally yielded by Nabuchodonosor. Suppose God has shown to Baltassar—less publicly perhaps but with equal insistence and cogency—signs of His Truth, His Unity, His Power. There is the struggle, then, in Baltassar's soul between God and not-God (we never hear of Baltassar paying court to Bel or Nebo or Marduk or any of the other local gods ; inscriptions that have praised Nabonidus's piety are silent about the Regent's devotional life) . . . with the result that once

brave with liquor, and having decided once for all to
stifle the call of grace, Baltassar shows—perhaps more
to the satisfaction of his own mind than of anyone
else's—the completest contempt for the things of God.
He does so (I would therefore suggest) not because he
denies their sacred character but because he believes
in it.   Nabuchodonosor's weakness, until the final
turning-point was reached, lay in relapse after conviction ; Baltassar's weakness lies in flight.   The one
faced God and, when the mood had left him, turned
away ; the other turns away and, when he is not sober,
faces God.

This is the place to say why Daniel (in my very
fallible opinion) has made no mention of anything that
has taken place in his or anybody else's affairs between
Nabuchodonosor's return to sanity and Baltassar's ill-
fated banquet.   Daniel was an artist, and he *wanted*
us to make some such comparison between the two
kings.   He wanted the Baltassar story to come on top
of the Nabuchodonosor story because they both meant
the same thing ;[1] or, rather, because each pointed to
the same truths from its own, very different, angle.
The conflict was the same in both men's souls, it was
only in the results of the conflict that the contrast was
intended to be seen.   The Baltassar story is virtually
over by the time you have reached the fourth verse ;
the rest of the tale is magnificent, dramatic in the
extreme, charged with supernatural meaning, enlighten-
ing in many ways, and full of historical interest, but the
moral of the whole thing lies (I feel) in the short recital
of what took place before the unearthly fingers started
writing on the wall.   And what did the moral imply ?
Why, surely that where the reason of the one man was

[1] And because time, in any case, meant very little to Daniel.

restored by grace, the reason of the other was expelled
by sin ; that where the punishment of one was to live
among beasts, the punishment of the other was to be
one ; that where Nabuchodonosor loved too much the
things of God's creation, Baltassar feared too much—
and then hated—the God who had created them. . . .

But I may be quite wrong about this. It is quite
possible that there was nothing very noteworthy in
the reigns of Evil-Merodach, Neriglissar, Labashi-
Marduk, and the first sixteen years of Nabonidus,
and that *therefore* Daniel spared his pen ; it is quite
possible that the Prophet was so much occupied in
administration—the men at the head being utterly
useless—that he had no leisure for the work of writing ;
it is quite possible that Daniel was living in the strictest
retirement all those years, and was receiving those
visions which make the material of his central chapters
(vii–xii) . . . all these contingencies are quite
possible—probable even—I am only saying what I
myself *think*.

> ' Then were the gold and silver vessels brought
> . . . and the king and his nobles and his wives
> and his concubines drank in them. They drank
> wine and praised their gods of gold and of silver,
> of brass, of iron, and of wood and of stone.'

One would have thought that even judged by
standards of Babylonian revelry this was carrying
things rather far. There seems, however, to have been
no demur on the part of the guests. Strong liquor is
a universal leveller, and one can only suppose that
religious and even superstitious sensibilities were sunk
at that well-filled board. Political differences too,
which on a less convivial occasion would have appeared

K

in striking contrast, were evidently likewise forgotten.[1] Whatever were the sentiments of his guests at the beginning of the meal, the combined effect of Baltassar's many cups and many courses seems to have deadened any animosity that existed, so that by the time of the dessert there prevailed a spirit of unusually comprehensive benevolence. Baltassar's shortcomings as a general, as a legislator, as an economist were generously waved aside in this display of lavish hospitality. Here he was, the old scoundrel, caring nothing for God or man . . . he certainly knew how to entertain . . . adding novelty upon novelty to an epoch-making repast . . . not nearly so bad as he was painted . . . why, anything could be forgiven to so liberal a host as was rich, fat, riotous king Baltassar . . . and now might I trouble you for another of those salted almonds?

Baltassar is proposing a toast. The music has stopped and the dancers who have been performing before the guests have melted into the background. The trolleys that have done double service this evening —first bringing in food and then the sacred plate of Israel—have been wheeled out of sight against the wall. People are rising to respond to the king's toast. ' They drank wine and praised the gods of gold, of silver, of brass and of iron, and of wood and of stone.' All eyes are on the king as he stands, swaying slightly, calling upon his nobles to respect the deities of the insensible.

[1] We must remember that the three preceding reigns (four, if we include the rule of the inept Nabonidus) had witnessed growing discontent, and had followed one another on reactionary waves. It is not unlikely that there were a fair number of nobles at that dinner who would gladly have dragged Baltassar's body, dead, from the place of honour.

iii

No preacher who has ever taken the danger of self-indulgence for his subject could be expected to resist the opportunity which this last-quoted verse of Daniel supplies. Surely there must be many an advocate of total abstinence who has lingered here for consolation. The connexion is so marked between ' drinking wine ' and ' praising the gods of gold and silver ' that one can almost see, as one looks down the centuries, the heavy scoring of these lines with the cold hard pencil of Puritanism. But even now, at a time when ebriety has managed to become more or less fashionable, the passage must surely have its thrust. Does not every form of self-indulgence incline to a lowering of the values—and that almost at once ? Baltassar's guests may not have been particularly God-fearing at the best of times, but once filled with the good things of this world they had no fear of ' praising ' what they knew would not be found in the next. All of us have to praise *someone*, and if we know we are being unfaithful to the One Who is worthy of praise the tendency is to praise the next best thing . . . even if the next best thing happens to be at the opposite extreme. And to Baltassar's pleasure-loving friends the next best things were quite definitely, the things ' of gold and silver.' Had the dinner been attended by artists, scientists, university dons, and heads of the legal and medical professions, and had these gentlemen indulged themselves to excess, then the case would doubtless have been different and the verse before us would have read : ' they drank wine and praised the gods of Beauty, of Progress, of Learning, of Good Order and of Health.'

But Baltassar's tables were not lined with the intelligentsia of Babylon. The people who came to his dinner were those who happened to be rich. They were other, and slightly lesser, Baltassars : they were bluff bucolics who worshipped success. They did not even worship breeding, they worshipped—the word is Daniel's—'brass.'[1]

To turn again from the table in question to the pulpit in general, is not every selfish pleasure, indulged in deliberately and without reference to God, followed almost immediately (we repeat) by a withdrawal from the heights ? It is not that we ever say, in so many words, ' I choose to be of the earth, earthy ; give me earthiness ' ; no, it is rather that we allow ourselves a little earthiness first, and then—partly to justify some secret claim within us, and partly also because our perceptions have been ever so slightly brutalised by what we have allowed—we turn upon our ' better selves ' with scorn. We drag our old ideals into the frosty sunshine of common sense . . . and laugh at them. Not the God of Israel, not the gods even of Babylon, but the god which goes by the names of Gold, of Iron and of Brass. The pitying superiority over ancient enthusiasms—seen in those who have lost the

---

[1] One ventures to think, incidentally, that the unexpected inclusion of ' iron,' ' wood,' and ' stone ' among the substances whose gods were honoured (' of gold and silver and of brass ') is to be accounted for by looking at Baltassar's condition rather than at the ingenious applications of the commentators. I would suggest therefore that the nobles did not vest the genius of wood- and stone-carving, etc., with a supernatural character, but simply that Baltassar trailed off into facetiousness. The toast-master makes his considered contribution, and then has nothing very much to say. The praise of gold and silver is *meant;* the rest is not. A paraphrase of the speech might be : ' Here's to the things that really matter in life, wealth, possessions, trade, and . . . er . . . a number of other things as well . . . like, say, marble bathing-ponds and log fires in the winter ' (sits).

poetry of religion and of youth—is one of the saddest things that a man can come across.

This has been an unwarrantable digression. It is what I feel when I read that ' they drank wine ' (in which by itself there was nothing wrong), and that they ' praised the gods of gold and silver ' (in which there was).

iv

Let us resume the story at the point where the sacred vessels were laid down, empty, upon the tables.

> ' In the same hour there appeared fingers, as it were, of the hands of a man, writing over against the candle-stick upon the surface of the wall of the king's palace ; and the king beheld the joints of the hand that wrote. Then was the king's countenance changed and his thoughts troubled him, and the joints of his loins were loosed, and his knees struck one against the other.'

We are told of the effect which the writing had upon the king ; we are left to guess the effect which the king's ' countenance ' had upon the diners. The ' thousand nobles ' would have seen Baltassar's skin whiten and his jaw drop ; they would have heard the crash of the golden cup upon the floor ; they would have followed the king's gaze to the opposite wall . . . where they would have seen strange letters that had not been there before. Clearly this was not just one more feature of the evening's entertainment ; nor was there room for the hope that Baltassar's constitution had failed, for once, in the struggle to keep pace with his appetite. There was something more in this than met the eye. Perhaps they had better be going.

The banquet hall seems to have emptied fairly soon, because we hear no more of the king's friends that night. Later on the royal body-guard will appear, but of the satellites who had enjoyed his dinner not one remained to see the evening through. Cannot we imagine the stampede ? Throwing precedent and ceremony to the winds, men and women would have been seen pressing their way through the great doors, seizing their cloaks, bundling themselves into their carriages—and away.[1] What a medley of sound ! The shouts which would bring sleepy attendants running to their masters ; the jingle of harness and the neighing of horses ; the cracking of whips, the stamping of hoofs, the shrill cries of command, the creaking of wheels and straining of shafts ; and then, finally, the confused racket as the courtyard emptied itself in a disorderly rush.

Within the palace, meanwhile, ' the king cried out aloud to bring in the wise men, the Chaldeans, and the soothsayers.' So Baltassar has pulled himself together and is shouting for his magicians : how like his ' father ' ! Baltassar has no more idea of what the signs in front of him mean than Nabuchodonosor had any idea of what either of his dreams implied—summon the wise men !

The king was not left in solitary contemplation of the opposite wall for long. The magicians were shown in.[2] How incongruous these men must have looked,

[1] It seems that the custom of inviting women to banquets of this sort was not heard of in Babylon before this time. Only among the Persians was such a practice tolerated.

[2] They probably—like Nabuchodonosor's staff of wise men before them—had lodgings in the king's palace, or, if the garrison palace at Arkad was not large enough to house a resident community of magicians, they may have belonged to a travelling suite, ready to accompany Baltassar on his campaigns and always within hailing distance.

lined up in a row with their feet among the flutes and drums and fallen flagons of wine. . . .

' They could neither read the writing nor declare the interpretation.' We are told that Baltassar was ' much troubled ' at this—as well he might be—and that his ' countenance was changed.' What happened to the sorcerers we do not know. Being much exercised in mind Baltassar probably forgot to have them burnt or executed or cast to the lions ;[1] perhaps they asked leave to go out on to the roof for a little while in order to consult the stars ; perhaps they found their way to the kitchens, and spent the rest of the night splitting open doves with the hope of finding an answer in the entrails ; perhaps, abandoning all attempt to find a solution to the king's difficulty, they simply went off and had a cold supper somewhere. They do not appear in the story again.

The text goes on to say that the lords (the resident members, that is, of the king's court) ' also were troubled ' ; they probably felt that whatever evil there was in store for Baltassar was in store for themselves as well. The next thing to be done, they decided, was to tell the queen-mother what had happened : she, with her experience of previous courts (and their similar situations), would be sure to know if there was anyone who could be turned to in the present crisis. The ministers were not disappointed.

' The queen, on occasion of what had happened to the king and his nobles, came into the banquet-house, and she spoke and said : O king, live for ever ; let not thy thoughts trouble thee, nor let

---

[1] The fate of useless servants is a detail which Nabuchodonosor would not have neglected.

thy countenance be changed ; there is a man in
thy kingdom that hath the spirit of the gods in
him ; and in the days of thy father knowledge
and wisdom were found in him ; for king Nabuchodonosor appointed him prince of the wise men
. . . now therefore let Daniel be called for, and he
will tell the interpretation.'

Something, clearly, must be said about this queen.
She is assumed to have been—and the text assists the
theory—Nabuchodonosor's widow. She need not have
been of a very great age at the time of the banquet
because she had probably married young and Nabuchodonosor had only been dead twenty years. The reason
why she is made out to have been Baltassar's great-
grandmother and not his grandmother is because
Nabonidus's mother (and therefore Baltassar's grandmother) is known from inscriptions to have died eight
years previously.[1]   If the assumption regarding the
queen's identity be correct then her name was Nictocris,
and she is believed to have controlled the kingdom's
finances for some considerable time after her husband's
death.   According to Herodotus she did her best to
stave off the Persian invasion by laying her vast
private fortune at the disposal of the State. Small
wonder that the nobles knew where to turn when in
a difficulty ; queen Nictocris must have been the most
capable of women. Whether or not the legends are

---

[1] I have seen the relationship worked out on paper and it seemed,
for one luminous moment, to fit in perfectly with all the possibilities
mentioned at the beginning of this chapter. I should waste a great
deal of space were I to try and recapture that moment here.   Dr
Charles (op. cit., pp. 126–9) is worth reading on the point, since he
gives what the historians have thought about it ; he wisely does not
commit himself, however, to any one view.

true connecting her name with the attempts within the capital to keep aflame the spirit of nationalism which her husband had originally kindled, certain it is that she had managed to keep in touch with the leading figures of the *ancien régime* rather than mix with the ever-changing personnel of succeeding courts. Daniel, at all events, the handsome hero of the dowager-queen's memories, had been kept in mind as a friend to be relied upon. Had he not been of invaluable service to Nabuchodonosor ? That young man's career should have been followed up ! Let Daniel be sent for ! He was not a young man any longer ? Perhaps not ; he was almost the same age as the queen herself ; no matter, Daniel was the man for to-night's work. . . . The king nodded assent to the proposal ; after all he had nothing to lose and perhaps something to gain. The nobles withdrew ; the queen remained. There would be an hour or so to wait until the Prophet could be brought before the king ; there was plenty meanwhile to occupy the latter's mind.

Did Baltassar remember, one wonders, how the great Hebrew prophet, Isaias, had warned the world of Babylon's fall ?[1] Growing more sober every minute Baltassar must surely have recalled what he had learned as a child to dread : ' I will punish the king of Babylon and that nation, saith the Lord ' (were the words with which, almost in Baltassar's own time, another of Israel's prophets, Jeremias, had warned the

[1] How that Babylon's princes would rise from their feasting to defend the city (xxi), but in vain. How that—more explicitly still —Babylon had been told of pride and superstition which would prove her undoing : ' Thou hast said : I shall be a lady for ever . . . I shall not sit as a widow, and I shall not know barrenness. These two things shall come upon thee *in one day*, barrenness and widowhood . . . because of the multitude of thy sorceries ' (Isaias xlvii, 5–14).

erring nation of its end), ' and I will make it perpetual
desolations.'[1]

v

We have no information as to where Daniel was
living at this time. It is unlikely that he had come
into personal contact with the court during Baltassar's
reign or there would have been no need for the introduction which we read of as having taken place on his
arrival. ' Art thou Daniel,' was the king's opening
remark, ' whom my father the king brought out of
Judea ? I have heard of thee that thou hast the spirit
of the gods.' The mention of the ' gods ' was not a
tactful one. ' And now the wise men and magicians
have come in before me,' went on the king, ' to read
this writing and to show me the interpretation
thereof, and they could not declare to me the meaning
of this writing. But I have heard of thee that thou
canst interpret obscure things . . . now if thou art
able to read the writing and show me the interpretation
thereof, thou shalt be clothed with purple and shalt
have a chain of gold about thy neck and shalt be the
third prince in my kingdom.'

Let us pause here for a moment and review the scene
as it must have appeared to Daniel while Baltassar
was making his complimentary speech. At his entry
into the hall the Prophet would have noticed the signs
of what had evidently been a very festive assembly :
the scattered fruits, the flagons of wine, the litter of
orchestral apparatus, and—more serious by far—the
desecrated vessels of the Lord. He would also have

<hr>

[1] Jeremias xxv, 12.

recognised queen Nictocris.[1] Indeed he had probably judged that it was on account of that lady's partiality towards himself that he had been dragged from his bed at such an hour ; it was not likely that Baltassar was merely wanting someone to talk to when his guests had gone. Daniel, moreover, would have taken good stock of the king's appearance ; which was far from pleasing.

Daniel would have noticed all these things, but what he would not have noticed—because it was behind his head—was the writing on the wall which he had been summoned to explain. It was Baltassar who drew the Prophet's attention to the wall which faced the royal couch. With the last-quoted words before us, I put forward the following reconstruction :

At Baltassar's mention of the ' writing,' Daniel turns round ; the rest of the king's speech is addressed to Daniel's back. Baltassar, who sees that the Prophet is reading ' the thing that is come to pass ' (and wanting above all things to keep on the right side of the one man in the kingdom who is likely to be of any use to him) goes on breathlessly to speak of the rewards he is prepared to offer. ' Thou shalt be clothed with purple ; thou shalt have a chain of gold about thy neck ; thou shalt be third prince in my kingdom.' And between each clause we seem to hear the beating of the king's heart !

' To which Daniel made answer and said before the king : Thy rewards be to thyself ' (the Prophet has turned back again by now, and what he has to say

---

[1] Is it possible, as some have thought, that the queen was ' under instruction ' to be received into the Faith that Nabuchodonosor had finally professed ? There is nothing impossible in the suggestion except that her reference to the ' spirit of the holy gods ' would in that event have been somewhat out of place.

' before the king ' is flung at Baltassar across the room), ' and the gifts of thy house give to another ; but the writing I will show to thee, O king, and show to thee the interpretation thereof.' The Bible is felt to tingle in one's hands ! The language of moral indignation does not alter with time and nationality : You can keep your bribes . . . go and give your presents to someone else. If you want me to tell you what those words mean, it's this. . . . And the Prophet proceeds to tell it.

How different is this from the breaking of bad news to Nabuchodonosor. The bad news, as Daniel broke it, was as follows :

' O king, the most high God gave to Nabuchodonosor thy father a kingdom, and greatness, and honour and glory,'—the speaker is beginning his announcement with a brief biographical survey touching the manner of the ancestor's reaction to grace—' and for the greatness that He gave to him, all people, tribes and languages trembled and were afraid of him ; whom he would he slew, and whom he would he destroyed ; and whom he would he set up and whom he would he brought down. But when his heart ‘was lifted up and when his spirit hardened into pride, he was put down from the throne of his kingdom and his glory was taken away. And he was driven out from the sons of men, and his heart was made like the beasts, and his dwelling was with the wild asses, and he did eat grass like an ox, and his body was wet with the dew of heaven, *till he knew that the Most High ruled in the kingdom of men. . . .*' Now Baltassar knew that all this had happened to his relative ; Daniel intended, however, that the implications as they affected the present king's case should be clearly underlined. Your father (says Daniel in effect) learned the lesson at a cost : it is a pity you have not benefited by the price he paid.

' Thou also his son, O Baltassar,' the Prophet goes on, ' hast not humbled thy heart whereas thou knewest these things, but hast lifted up thy heart against the Lord of heaven '—does not this bear out the suggestion that Baltassar knew Who the Lord of heaven *was*, and that he had resisted Him ? ' And the vessels of His house have been brought before thee, and thou and thy wives and thy nobles have drunk wine in them ; and thou hast praised the gods of silver and of gold and of brass and of iron and of wood and of stone, that neither see nor hear nor feel ; *but the God Who hath thy breath in His hand . . . thou hast not glorified.*'

It is a magnificent indictment. We notice at once that the sins which Daniel stresses most are the sins of omission—the worst sin of all being that of not giving glory to God. Perhaps the king had no need to be told of the positive evils of which he had been guilty : he knew them all already and may even, by this time, have been heartily contrite. The point which had to be put first in the list of Daniel's charges was the fact that pride lay at the root of all his—as of his father's—sins. He had only himself to blame, therefore, for the miseries that were to come.

' And this,' explains the Prophet at last, ' is the writing that is written : MANE, THECEL, PHARES. And this is the interpretation of the word : MANE, God hath numbered thy kingdom and hath finished it ; THECEL, thou art weighed in the balance and art found wanting ; PHARES, thy kingdom is divided and given to the Medes and Persians.'

The dreadful revelation could hardly have been put more shortly. We read of no further explanation from the lips of Daniel. We can only conclude that the Prophet bowed, withdrew, and went home the way he came . . . to pray for the people who were to die that day. There was no appeal to Baltassar's better self : no suggestion that sins might be redeemed with alms-giving and redress. This was surely not because Daniel doubted the existence of a ' better self ' in Baltassar ; a much more likely reason for not mentioning the question of reparation and restitution seems to me to be that he knew there was no time for either. Even as he had been speaking, the first word ' MANE : the kingdom is finished ' had been fulfilled—the streets of Babylon were running with blood. The empire had slipped from the grasp of Babylon's king.

' THECEL : thou art wanting in the scales ' . . . that too—this very evening—had been amply justified. Even a Lord Who had blessed Baltassar and his ante-cedents with a generosity which, had it been found in man, would have been counted for extravagance, even *He* must take the testimony of the balance. To the eternal credit of Baltassar it must be said that he, likewise, accepted the witness of that balance. He seems to have decided then and there to use what little was left to him of time and authority (before the third word ' PHARES : thy kingdom is given to the Medes and Persians ' should come into operation) to carry out what he had promised. ' Then by the king's command Daniel was clothed with purple, and a chain of gold was put about his neck ; and it was proclaimed of him that he had power as the third man in the kingdom.'

As to how much use the Prophet was able to make of this last honour the next two verses of the text enable us to guess. Scripture closes the Baltassar incident as follows :

' The same night Baltassar the Chaldean king was slain.'

An inglorious end ? Not altogether. In fact not necessarily at all. If one of the man's last acts was to make good his position with a fellow man, may we not hope that *the* last act was to make good his position with Almighty God ?[1]

[1] I am writing this quite indefensible footnote in the Babylonian Room of the British Museum.

Having occasion to pass through London, and feeling at the same time that the walls of Babylon are crumbling under Persia's weight (within earshot, almost, of Paddington Station), I have decided to spend the best part of the day in this luminous crystal of the past. For some hours now I have been inspecting the relics of the age which we have been considering in this book. Shamelessly I have wrung every ounce of emotional value from the many objects which relate to our period (and before). Such conduct has always appeared to me thoroughly degrading (like putting on a gramophone record to recapture a memory), and I only excuse myself in this instance by reason of the fact that I came here this morning out of a stern sense of duty and with the interests of cold hard history at heart. But the romance of the Babylonian Room has won me over.

There must be a number of things here on which Daniel's eyes have actually rested. There is certainly a six-foot bronze step on which Nabuchodonosor's foot has rested. (This step comes from the palace at Birs-Nimrod, and bears on one side the inscription which fixes its date. Nabuchodonosor had it put at the entry of the local temple which he had built in the honour of Nebo. It shows a simple *répoussé* design which has suffered surprisingly little from the wear of worshipping feet ; perhaps the temple was approached by another door ; or perhaps there was not a great number of worshippers.) The excavations of 1927-8 among the graves at Ur (some two hundred miles south of Babylon) have made it possible for us to reconstruct more of Babylonian life than has been possible hitherto. And not only the Babylonian life which was lived in the centuries before us, but also that which considerably preceded Daniel's date. For instance, I have just been looking at some Chaldean ornaments which belong to the early Sumerian Period, 3000 B.C. ; these were museum pieces a good thousand years before Nabuchodonosor was born—and the colours as fresh as the Sutton's flower-beds which flashed past me this morning as I came up in the train. Necklaces, brooches, gold cups, wine-strainers, wig-helmets, lyre-frames, table ornaments, pins of one kind and another, rings and what not. . . . This room must be the Mecca of Babylonian students all the world over. A man can sit (as I am sitting—on the attendant's stool) within reach of a goblet that was probably used at Baltassar's banquet. I admit it frankly, I am in a world that is very far indeed from Russell Square. I hear the flapping of sandalled feet over flagged pavements. . . . I smell the strange scents of the bazaar.

That brick on the shelf to my right, what has it not seen of Babylonian pageantry and drama ? It is stamped with Nabuchodonosor's name and looks like a rather massive dog biscuit. It has probably witnessed the Dedication Procession to and from the Plain of Dura ; it has probably seen the arrival, as convoy followed convoy, of king Joakin with his fellow-captives from Jerusalem ; it has probably looked down upon Nabuchodonosor's legionaries as they went off to fight their sovereign's battles for him ; it has probably heard the whispered consultations of the wise men, who, walking always in the fear of death, would have hugged the sheltering walls of street and palace ; and Daniel may have passed within a yard of it when he was hurried through the sleeping city on his way to meet the summons of Baltassar. . . .

But an exhibit which must be of interest to more than just the few Daniel enthusiasts is the mosaic fragment which stands, alone in its glory, on a polished mahogany pedestal. It shows a file of nobles and soldiers in silhouette. It is the direct lineal ancestor of the Bayeux Tapestry, the Carpaccio procession paintings, and the low relief friezes that run round countless war memorials in England to-day. When the little pieces of white and blue were laid alongside one another Abraham had not yet considered the question of moving across the desert into Western Asia. In fact if Abraham was born in 2160 B.C. it gives him an easy margin of several hundred years before he need think of leaving Ur of the Chaldees. 2085 B.C. is the date given by Sir Charles Marston (in his delightful book, *The Bible Comes Alive*) as being roughly the time of Abraham's entry into Canaan.

I am being looked at (a shade reproachfully, it seems to me) by a little Chaldean goddess. She must have been a winning creature in her day. Clean, white, four inches high and exquisitely proportioned, she looks as if she has just fallen out of a very expensive cracker. She is four thousand five hundred years old if she is a day ! No wonder she resents—with all that tradition behind her—the cheap journalism which she knows I am indulging in at her expense.

From this my fancy takes a further flight, and I ask myself how many Europeans—apart from how many Babylonians—have gazed at these objects and have been gazed at in return ? What number of anæmic clergymen, for instance, have sat in front of my brick (the one which should be tried on the dogs that are waiting outside for their masters), or else shuffled past in search of the even more spectacular trophies which await one in the Egyptian Room next door ? I can see them all (all these clerical pilgrims) as clearly as I can see the priests of Babylon . . . this one is preparing what will prove to be, after Herculean labours, a lecture of incredible dullness ; another has come, catalogue in hand, to verify a footnote which is worrying him ; another is here to make a little sketch ; another to shelter, merely, from the rain . . . and, last of all, myself.

Perhaps it is due to this curious tendency which reveals itself when one visits museums (the tendency I have just been yielding to—that of living in at least two worlds at once) that the attendants wear the expressions which they do. In no museum in England— and certainly in no museum abroad—are there to be found men more courteous or better informed than these of the British Museum. Something, however, of the measured course of ages seems to have communicated itself to the faces of these men. Their faces are sad and grey and still ; they remind one of abandoned slate quarries. These men have seen too much of history ; or rather they have seen too much of both ends and not enough of the middle. Not every man can pass easily from the presence of one of Sargon's winged bulls to his modest luncheon in Montague Street. The ordinary mind finds it difficult to be continually answering questions and giving directions as to the whereabouts of such and such a glass case, when at the same time it is living in a land peopled by prin- cesses of the Hittite or Sumerian periods. Between these things there is fixed a great gulf—a ' chaos ' ; to be for ever bridging such chasms must make for greyness, sadness, stillness. The sunshine of distant centuries no longer glows in the skins of those best placed to bask in it. A solemn travesty if ever there was one.

Later : at the Cenacle Convent, Grayshott, where I am about to give a retreat.

I must apologise for the way in which this footnote is taking upon itself the character of a diary ; I can only say that this sort of thing will not occur again : one cannot visit a museum twice in the same book. All that I want to add to the above is merely this : that I was wrong, of course, when I compared the British Museum to Mecca ; it is much more like Lourdes. One comes away with the same feeling of exhilaration which one experiences on leaving the Grotto. One could comfortably hang up a crutch in the Babylonian Room of the British Museum. One feels a happier and an improved (in the sense of a better instructed) man. But then one is not an attendant.

CHAPTER IX

THE PROPHET UNDER DARIUS
(Daniel v, 31–vi, 2.)

i

' And Darius the Mede succeeded to the kingdom, being threescore and two years old . . .
and he appointed over the kingdom a hundred
and twenty governors to be over his whole kingdom, and three princes over them, of whom Daniel
was one.'

THE nomination of Darius as Baltassar's (or
Nabonidus's) successor is perhaps a surprise to us
when it is Cyrus whom we have been expecting to take
up the reins. The answer seems to be that Cyrus had no
time to attend to his latest annexation, and so appointed
a general who had been with him in his previous campaigns. The man Darius has been identified with a
number of more or less contemporary figures ; if his
lifetime covered the lifetimes of all the people to whom
his identity has been assigned he would have enjoyed
some two hundred years of life. The matter need not
detain us here ; all that should be noted is that the
Darius mentioned in the text is not the Darius the
Great (Hystaspes) who married Cyrus's daughter and
reigned over the Persian Empire from 521–485 B.C.
The Darius of Daniel's story *may* have been Cyrus's

right-hand man Gobryas (who certainly entered
Babylon on the night of the fall), but to make him out
to have been either Artaxerxes, Xerxes, or even
Cambyses II (who died as early as 521 and therefore
might have been in some sort of official position at the
time we are considering) is surely borrowing too much
from the future. When we are told that Daniel's
' Darius the Mede ' was probably not a Mede at all,
and that ' Darius ' was almost certainly not his
name, we may be permitted in a study of this sort to
pass on . . . wondering, merely, at the marvellous
wit of man. *Someone*, a petty king or governor, was
given (at the age of sixty-two) the care of Babylon.
The giver of this throne was Cyrus.[1] Cyrus, we must
remember, was rapidly becoming master of the then
known world ; quite likely, therefore, would have been
the entrusting of Babylon and all its dependencies to a
subordinate. It should be remarked here that the
taking of Babylon, significant as the triumph was,
would hardly have ranked as one of Cyrus's more signal
conquests : fully half of Baltassar's Babylon fell ready
victims into the hands of the conqueror. Perhaps if the
Chaldeans had put up a stouter resistance, Cyrus himself would have remained in the capital after he had
taken it. One wishes that the Bible text were less
economical in its record of historical events. It would
be interesting to know, for instance, whether Baltassar's
death was the work of a Mede, a Persian, or a Babylonian malcontent. It seems unthinkable that even a

[1] This period of Babylon's history is fully dealt with in Professor
Lods' book, *The Prophets and the Rise of Judaism*, under the section
which treats of the Jews and the Persian domination. I have not
assumed the identifications here (choosing rather to abide by the
stricter commentators), but the whole work, even if the writer's
conclusions are not always acceptable to Catholics, is worthy of
careful study. See also Pope (pp. 359–364) and Driver (p. 70).

percentage of the Chaldean people, with the blood of
Babylon in its veins, should welcome the invader.
How is it that the yoke of Persia should be preferred
to the indolent rule of Baltassar ?   One can only
suppose that the answer lies deeper than in a widespread exasperation at the moribund foreign policy of
the last half-dozen years ; looked at from this distance
it is impossible to find satisfactory reasons for the
reactionary movements of a people vastly different
from our own, but it is worth bearing in mind that
ever since the days of Nabuchodonosor's rule in Babylon
(when that king had dictated to the nation what gods
they were to serve—and finally when he had discarded
all gods in favour of the God of Israel) discontent in
matters religious had been considerably on the increase.
It is believed that during Baltassar's ill-starred period
of power the risings which had been successfully
quashed during previous reigns became both more
frequent and more frenzied.   Baltassar's mode of life
must have stung the zealots to an almost fanatical
thirst for reform.   Thus the devotees of the suppressed
or neglected deities[1] saw in the Cyrus invasion—with
its indifference to Chaldean forms of worship—a possible
return to the old order of things.   Isaias had not been
mistaken when he had cried out, years before, that
' the partakers of graven things shall assemble together
and shall say to Cyrus : Thou art our shepherd.'[2]

It would be fascinating to embark here upon a long
digression about Cyrus the Persian.   He must have been

---

[1] Nabuchodonosor had relegated Ninip, Nebo, Beltis, Gula, and
the gods of the sun and moon to what corresponded to the Pantheon
in Babylon.   And this had distressed his subjects considerably.
Nabonidus was devout, but he was at the same time so inept as to
do little for the cause of religion in Babylon.

[2] Isaias xliv, 11-28.

as interesting a person as Nabuchodonosor. The connexion, however, between Cyrus and the Book of Daniel is only accidental (unless Cyrus is the king who is mentioned in the famous fourteenth chapter which gives the stories of Bel and the dragon) and so we feel hardly justified in saying very much about him. Nevertheless a paragraph about his policy is required, even if his individuality is left to the imagination, otherwise it will be impossible to see how Daniel had any place in the new dispensation . . . or why it was that Darius was to be so easily twisted round the thumbs of his subordinates.

Isaias foretold the career of Cyrus in glowing terms : ' Thus saith the Lord to My anointed Cyrus, whose right hand I have taken hold of to subdue the nations before his face ; for the sake of My servant I have called him by name.'[1] Cyrus was raised up, then, in order to further the fortunes of the Chosen People. In the event it was certainly owing to the tolerance of this king that the Hebrew people were able to assemble their scattered energies and to concentrate upon the re-establishment at Jerusàlem. It would be a mistake, however, to look upon Cyrus at this stage as a devout monotheist whose one aim was to restore the Faith to the Jewish people ; more than anything else he was a dexterous diplomatist. From the outset Cyrus had decided that it would be a good thing to have all gods —Chaldean, Israelite, and any other—re-enshrined. Later on he may or may not have come to the belief in the One True God ; at the time which concerns us he was, for purely political reasons and also because he was not an extremist in matters religious, allowing his colonists to go home. So large were his conquests

[1] Isàias xlv, 1–4.

that he was able to emancipate whole nations. Those
of his subjects who were exiles and who at the same
time had no desire to return to the lands of their birth
were at perfect liberty to remain on ; they might
worship whom they would ; they might even regard
themselves as eligible where important positions of
state were concerned. Thus wherever Cyrus's influence
penetrated it soon became clear that the policy of
Persia was one of toleration ; so long as he and his
deputies remained in supreme power, the dictator was
for following (within certain clearly defined limits)
the traditional lines that had been laid down before he
had appeared in the field. Hence the native officials
under Darius. Hence, also, the fact that Daniel was
among them.

ii

The *lacunæ* in Daniel's account of his life are heart-
breaking to his biographers ; the episode which is made
by the Prophet to follow that of Baltassar's banquet
can hardly have taken place within five years of that
event (some think later still). The story which we
have to consider in this chapter—the story of the lion's
den—will require to be treated in some detail ; it is
not only significant in itself but it also needs to be
differentiated from another incident connected with
lions and dens—a story which will be dealt with later
on, and which belongs to another period altogether.
But before we pick up the narrative it will be necessary
to note the effect produced upon the Jews in Babylon
by those liberative measures which we have been
considering in the previous section.

Taking first the Hebrew who most nearly concerns
us, Daniel himself, we can hardly be wrong in thinking

that the Prophet spent the decade or so after the fall
of Babylon in trying to shepherd his fellow-exiles into
a flock sufficiently homogeneous to enable them to
form a politico-religious body which should be worthy
of serious consideration on the part of the authorities.
And if this was the case it seems equally clear that the
Prophet failed in his endeavour.   Strange, we think,
that Daniel with all his wisdom, and with the free hand
that was being allowed him by Cyrus, should have made
so little impression. . . . Let us approach the thing
from the other angle and look at the Jews whom he was
trying to influence.

At the beginning of the Captivity (seventy years ago)
the exiles had been urged by their prophet, the great
Jeremias, to settle down and make the best of it.
' Build ye houses and dwell in them,' had been the
instructions of God's mouthpiece, ' plant orchards and
take ye wives . . . be ye multiplied there and be ye
not few in number.   And seek ye the peace of the
city. . . .'[1]   And in doing all this the Jews had been
only too successful : they had built very permanent
dwellings indeed and were in no mood to leave them ;
they had planted orchards and were enjoying the fruit ;
they had sought the peace of the city and were resting
in blissful content.   The Hebrew has a way of attracting
to himself the good things of this world, and doubtless
even here in Babylon the children of the dispersion
were the children of acquisition.   We must remember
that Babylon had no particular quarrel with Jerusalem :
the Captivity had been brought about—in the first
instance—by war with the nation to which Juda had
the misfortune to be subject.   As time went on, and
urged by their religious leaders to give edification and

[1] Jeremias xxix, 5, 6, 7.

not trouble to those responsible for order in the city,
the Jews found themselves amassing fortunes, acquiring
civic dignity, establishing social contacts . . . *and*,
naturally enough, forgetting all about Jerusalem.[1]
After all there was much to be said for the land of
their adoption : Chaldea was no less pleasant a part of
the world to live in than Palestine . . . yes, the seventy
years—for all the home-sickness at the start—had
flown ; the practice of the true religion had, after a
fashion, been kept up ; prophets had never been lacking
to show them, if they cared to look, which was the way
to follow. . . . In the event it had been stimulating

---

[1] As a matter of history we find that, though the Jews have
always been a hated race, they have had little difficulty in adapting
themselves to the lives and manners of those with whom they have
had to ' sojourn.' You have only to look at the three centuries
which preceded the coming of Christ to see the effect which the
Jews managed to produce upon the civilizations which were then
to the front. Pogroms only became popular when the nations that
resorted to them had turned round to find that their money was
pouring into Jewish coffers. (The attitude of Germany to-day is not
a unique one.) Somehow or other we seem to associate the breaking
up of Hebrew unity with the destruction of the Temple (and fall
of Jerusalem) as foreshadowed by Our Lord. But other temples
had been destroyed before then ; other Jerusalems had fallen. By
the time of Christ, as a fact, three hundred years had passed since
the Great Diaspora. In Our Lord's day there were Jewish colonies
in all the big cities of the world ; and tolerably contented colonies
they were. It is true that the synagogue in Alexandria had fared
none too well from the outset, but in Athens, Antioch, and Rome it
flourished. Nowhere was there any move to stamp out the Jew.
In fact the Jew seems in these cities to have escaped ostracism as
well as persecution : in Apostolic times we find a powerful Jewish
influence at the head of shipping, banking, and trading interests.
It was this universal spread that, of course, facilitated (though
unintentionally) the carrying of the Gospel over the civilized world.
Further, if it can be said that the Hebrews ingratiated themselves
within the walls of capitals, it is equally true to say that they
managed as successfully in the rural dominions of those under whose
flag they ' tarried.' In such patches of colonization, for instance,
as Crete and Cyprus and Rhodes. Before and after the coming of
Christ the histories of the many ' dispersions ' have always been
the same : unobtrusive burrowing . . . gradual accumulating . . .
and then finally—but only after a very long time as a rule—trouble.

rather than enervating (so the Jews would have argued themselves into believing) to have lived all this time with unbelievers : it had quickened their trust in Jehovah. . . . Always to feel, moreover, that there was a homecoming to which they could look forward had added a certain warmth to life, something to cling to on those rare occasions when they would be reminded of the fact that they were a race apart.

But now that the return to Jerusalem was imminent, now that having to say good-bye to houses, orchards, and friends was actually a question of practical moment, the picture was beginning to take on a slightly different tone. Once back in the Holy City (the ' exiles ' must have reminded themselves) they would be strangers to their co-religionists ; they would be out of date ; they would, with their heathen mannerisms, be looked upon with suspicion and considered rather gauche ; the awkwardness which they would inevitably display in the hundred and one little observances which they would be expected to practise (and which, heaven knew, they had been justified enough in ' forgetting ') would excite remark ; their children's Chaldean accent would be made fun of at school ; their own learning (good of its kind and expensively bought—Babylonian degrees were well worth having) would be despised. The manners, the clothes, and even the wives of the returning exiles would be objects of vulgar and slightly supercilious curiosity in the city of David . . . could they not remain in Babylon, and things go on just as they were ?

It was this kind of thing that Daniel had to deal with.

Far harder than divining dreams or cursing kings was the task of Daniel in the years that followed Cyrus's conquest. Staying on himself, he had to tell the Jews to go away. He knew that the seventy years which had been decreed by God were nearly up. The gates of Babylon stood open. The ruins of the Holy City were calling out for a Holy People to repair its walls . . . and dwell within them for ever. And the Lord willed that Israel should fold up her tents once more: ' Remove out of the midst of Babylon, and go forth out of the land of the Chaldeans, and be ye as kids at the head of the flock.'[1] The thing was as clear (alas) as the Decalogue.

We do not know for certain what it was that decided Daniel's choice to stay behind. Historians point out the duty of remaining at the elbow of so well-disposed a king (Darius) ; others see a need where the spiritual wants were concerned of those who refused, point-blank, to go ; again there was the chance, provided by the Prophet's rank, of introducing the true religion into Babylon. Daniel may be justified on many heads. Heavens, as if the man was not able to judge the will of God in his regard when nothing but grace had guided him for the last seventy years and more ! He prayed about it, and elected *not* to join the home-going caravans. Presumably he received the light to choose as he did. There is no more to add. That Daniel was not able, banner in hand, to lead a chanting procession through the desert—but rather had to push a sullen people from behind—is to his glory, not his shame. There is a glamour about the veteran Prophet putting fire into the hearts of the Chosen People and beckoning to them as he strides out of the western gate of Babylon. But glamour must be left behind in the way to God. To us who are inclined to judge as ' carnal men, not spiritual ' there would perhaps seem nothing finer

[1] Jeremias l, 8.

than that an enlightened statesman should make the great renunciation and return, a humble pilgrim, to his spiritual home. Perhaps this is just what Daniel would have liked to do. Perhaps this was the big temptation of his life. We do not know. But just as it was not granted to Moses to lead the Chosen People into the Land of Promise, so it was not granted to Daniel to lead them back to it. In the case of Moses it was, we are told, largely his fault : he was lacking in trust. In the case of Daniel it was not his fault at all. That is to say it was not because he had not trusted that he was kept away, it was rather because he had. His trust was being rewarded with a corresponding trust on the part of God.

Throughout the whole of his life Daniel had relied upon the extraordinary Providence of God to a quite extraordinary extent—and had found that his venture of faith had not, in any instance, been misplaced. Now he was to rely upon the quite ordinary Providence of God (if it can be called the ' ordinary ' Providence of God which assists a preacher to influence his people), and to be—for a time at least—disappointed.

' Look through the Bible,' says Cardinal Newman, ' and you will find God's servants, even though they begin with success, end with disappointment—not that God's purpose or instruments fail, but the time for reaping what we have sown is hereafter, not here ; and that there is no great visible fruit in any one man's lifetime.'[1] God's plan, then, is not necessarily being spoiled when man's effort to realise God's plan is found to come to nothing. God's plan *is* being spoiled, however, when His efforts to realise His plan in man's soul is found to come to nothing : when the will of

[1] *Parochial and Plain Sermons*, Vol. VIII, p. 129.

man, in other words, resists. *There* is failure—not God's, but man's.

To the disciple in the desert of Scete who obediently waters his master's staff (instead of the gourd that is growing alongside of his cell) there is something sufficiently mad about the whole thing to rob the exercise (perhaps) of the full bitterness of its humiliation. But to the elderly Prophet who waters his Master's withered shrub (and who hangs up his staff in the hall of his house) there is something sufficiently sad to make the whole business seem hardly worth while. Daniel, at this present stage in his career, was trying to coax the shrunken rose of Sharon back to life again. He failed.

' Offer to God,' is St Teresa of Lisieux's advice,[1] ' the sacrifice of never gathering any fruit off your tree . . . if He permits all the flowers of your desires and of your goodwill to fall on to the ground without any fruit appearing, do not worry. At the hour of death, in the twinkling of an eye, He will cause rich fruits to ripen on the tree of your soul.'

Not everyone is meant to carry weight with the world ; few people are intended to be successful ' moulders.' All that the individual has to make sure of is that he is prepared to carry *his* weight, that *he* is willing to be moulded. External contacts, the apostolate, suffering for others are all intended to stand the test of how they affect the soul of the individual concerned ; if they fail to bring out the particular ' likeness ' to God which is required they amount to nothing more than well-directed energies. In fact burdens—even holy burdens—not borne for God and

[1] Autobiography, *Counsels and Reminiscences*, p. 299.

having no directly correcting effect upon ourselves
are—quite simply—burdensome.

Daniel had need, if any man had, to know the truth
of all this. ' Go you out,' he was forced to say to the
Jews as he made his rounds, ' go you out, my children,
from among your friends and neighbours in this
Chaldea which you have learned to love as a native
land. Cross, I beg of you, those plains which separate
us from our Holy City. To you it is given to restore the
Law of God ; for you it is to build the Temple's fallen
walls ; to you is entrusted the inheritance of the
patriarchs of old ; your feet shall stand on holy
ground ; your voices shall be raised to the glory of
Jehovah's name. Go forth, my children, with the
blessing of God upon you . . . and I . . . well . . . I shall
be here to say good-bye.' How frightful it must have
been for Daniel to have had to say things like that.
How he must have waited for the horrid taunt which
sooner or later would be sure to fall from Hebrew lips
—' Go forth thyself.' How difficult it must have been
for him to keep his secret to himself, never disclosing
the fact that really he would be giving anything to
be one of them, but that as a matter of fact God wanted
something else from him. And if this shame and if this
secret were exceedingly mortifying to the Prophet,
how much more distressing to him would have been
the apathy of the Jews. Daniel was able to see how
enfeebling had been the effect of the ' seventy years '
upon the spirit of his people. Comfort had blinded
them to the promises of the Lord. The word of God
was no longer a living thing to them. Did the Prophet
in his exhortations to the downcast audiences which
it was his lot at this time to address, quote, I wonder,
from the Book of Sophonias ? ' The remnant of Israel

shall feed,' had that prophet (not so long ago) foretold,
' they shall lie down and there shall be none to make
them afraid. At that time when I will gather you I
will give you a name and praise among all the people
of the earth ; *when I have brought back your captivity
before your eyes*, saith the Lord.'[1] Daniel might well
have chosen those words for his text . . . but would
they have had any effect ? The Jews were paying
no attention to a living Prophet, why should they
have listened to a dead one ? The promises held out by
Sophonias would only have evoked the response that
here, in Chaldea, the remnant could ' feed and lie
down,' thank you, very comfortably . . . and that
few were apparent at the moment who showed the
least sign of ' making them afraid.' One weeps for
Daniel ; one must make excuses, too, for his people.
The Jews had lost the poetry of their lives : listless
were they, the ' seventy years ' had robbed them of
their flaming faith.

iii

The years which witnessed what we have presumed
to call Daniel's ' failure ' saw also the rise of two young
prophets who felt as Daniel did about the spinelessness
of Juda's sons. Aggeus and Zacharias were linked
with Daniel in their work for the Restoration. Aggeus
was chosen by God to hasten on the building of the
Temple in Jerusalem ; the Jews—such of them as
obeyed the Lord and returned to Palestine—were for
delaying the process indefinitely. ' Thus saith the
Lord of hosts,' was the warning of the prophet Aggeus,
' This people saith : The time is not come for the

[1] Sophonias iii, 13–20.

building of the house of the Lord. . . . Is it time for you,' the prophet asks, ' to dwell in ceiled houses and this house [the Temple] lie desolate ? Go up to the mountain ; bring timber and build the house.'[1] Zacharias, too, was becoming restive under this endless putting off. He addresses himself to the Lord : ' O Lord of hosts, how long wilt Thou not have mercy on Jerusalem and on the cities of Juda with which Thou hast been angry ? This is the seventieth year. . . .' And then the Prophet rounds upon the Jews that linger still in Babylon : ' Thus saith the Lord of hosts : I am zealous for Jerusalem with a great zeal, and I am angry with a great anger . . . O Sion, flee thou that dwelleth with the daughter of Babylon.'[2]

Unless we say (as we can have no scruple in saying) that this was all for the good of Daniel's soul, it is hard to explain why these two Minor Prophets were allowed to succeed where the Major Prophet failed. That the Minor Prophets did succeed we know : ' Then Zorobabel the son of Salathiel, and Jesus the son of Josedech the High Priest, and all the remnant of the people, hearkened to the voice of the Lord their God and to the words of Aggeus the prophet as the Lord their God sent him to them.'[3] No mention of Daniel. Daniel is under a cloud. Holy Scripture is silent about the part he played. Daniel is forgotten in the belated refounding. He will come into his own again in a little while, taking up the familiar *rôle* of hero, but for the present his work for souls is secret. We have seen how God sometimes keeps the fruit of His trees for Himself alone. With some souls He does more even than this ; He hides the growth. Notice how

---

[1] Aggeus i, 2, 4, 8. [2] Zacharias i, 12–15.
[3] Aggeus i, 12.

God kept the saint of Lisieux in littleness and not in flower : it was only afterwards that the capital letters were introduced, and men called her the Little Flower. St John of the Cross was never nearer to the Crucified than when he came to die, and yet his death was a very hidden event—with few to see how like his Lord he was. St Francis Xavier's death was much the same. The last years of St Jane Frances were a continual sorrow to her religious subjects for the apparent cooling of their mother's love !

'Having then so great a cloud of witnesses, let us run by patience to the fight proposed.'[1] 'The disciple is not above his master '[2] and we should be prepared, with Daniel, to forgo success. Such, at any rate, is the spirit of the saints ; they store up energy in obscurity. Like Moses, they learn most when in a cloud. We notice that Daniel's hiddenness had about it not even the glamour of disgrace, but only the cold, dull flatness of having failed. 'Failure' was after all the lot of Christ.

---

[1] Hebrews xii, 1.   [2] Matthew x, 24.

CHAPTER X

PERSONAL DEALINGS WITH DARIUS
(Daniel vi.)

i

THE rather jejune record of Daniel's declining
years has fortunately been filled out for us by
the Jewish historian Josephus. This writer is possessed
of a happy genius whereby he fastens upon the more
macabre aspect of any sensational occurrence which
comes his way; he colours history wherever he can
with the purple brush of an Edgar Allan Poe. Thus, if
it be objected that this chapter of plotters and bones
and agonised yells is overwritten, we can only point
to our authority—at once more trusted and more
near to the scene than we.

If not an octogenarian when called upon to face the
lions, Daniel must have been closer to eighty than
seventy. This is worth noting because to those of us
who are at all familiar with lithographic art, there
appear, in connexion with this incident, visions of a
radiant youth who is clad in a loose smock and is
belted about the waist with a be-jewelled band; the
picture includes beasts that have licked and purred
their way into the frame and who are expressing
either meek submission or rapt devotion; the beasts
are receiving—consciously—a benediction. A glance
over Daniel's shoulder and we see the background

to be a vast colosseum revealing tier upon tier of empty seats ; angels suffuse the scene with light.[1] We would merely observe in correcting this image that the place was a den and not a circus ; and that Daniel would have been the last person to approve of the falsification of his age to suit the claims of sentimentalism. But we are spoiling the story by beginning at the end.

> 'And the king [Darius] thought to set him [Daniel] over all the kingdom.'

It is clear that with the accession of Darius as Cyrus's deputy sovereign, Daniel was forced to play a more active part in the affairs of the realm than he had done in the reigns preceding ; this would account for the sudden expression of professional jealousy which had lain dormant in his fellow-ministers for so many years : ' Whereupon the princes and the governors sought to find occasion against Daniel with regard to the king ; and they could find no cause nor suspicion because he was faithful ; and no fault nor suspicion was found in him.' Darius had already given Daniel considerable authority and, as we have just seen, was thinking now of putting him in charge of a (surely it must be ' a ' and not ' the ') realm. And Daniel's

---

[1] Since writing the above I have come across two pictures which might have been painted to justify my objection. Both are by painters of the last century. The words which are printed below the reproduction of Vernet's picture run as follows : ' . . . serenely unmindful of danger, one of the lions in friendly companionship snuggled at his feet. This story is told to promote absolute reliance on the omnipotence of God.' The other picture is by an Englishman with a French name, Riviere. It gives, it is true, a slightly older Daniel than the one I have been complaining about, but it makes up for this by showing an even sweeter lion than anything I had thought possible when taking exception to the ' purring ' animals above.

colleagues (as well they might, seeing the Prophet was a foreigner) resented this.

> ' Then these men said : We shall not find any occasion against Daniel, unless perhaps concerning the law of his God.'

It is clear that Daniel's Jewish blood, even more than his advancement under Darius, was the cause of the anti-Daniel feeling at court. Men spoke of him as a Hebrew and a stranger : not even a refugee, but a child of the Captivity—a slave.

Thus, during one of Daniel's frequent absences from the capital,[1] a conclave was called by the malcontents, and a suitable way of ridding Babylon of Daniel was considered. The same sort of thing had doubtless been done before with regard to other prominent but unloved statesmen, and there was no reason why Daniel should not equally be disposed of. But where others had been caught on the thicket of indiscretion, Daniel's white cloak defied the thorn and barb. Some legal quibble must be hit upon which would twist the Hebrew from his seat of honour. The law was a safer weapon than mere calumny. (There had been that little matter of Susanna, you remember ; true, it had been a long time ago, but the elders had never quite regained the people's confidence ; the same mistake could not be made again . . . no, quite definitely, Daniel would have to be caught out this time on a question of jurisprudence.)

Having said good-bye to Daniel, then, the members of the king's privy council are discovered pleasantly

---

[1] The reason for thinking that Daniel was away is because Darius would surely, had the Prophet been at home, have consulted him about the matter in question when it was finally put before him.

occupied in framing a law which would get rid of the Prophet altogether. It is a pretty scene. ' The princes and governors craftily suggested to the king,[1] and spoke thus unto him : King Darius live for ever ; all[2] the princes of the kingdom, the magistrates, the governors, the senators, and the judges have consulted together that an imperial decree and an edict be published that whosoever shall ask any petition of any god or man for thirty days, but of thee, O king, shall be cast into the den of lions.' (It appears that the habit of keeping lions for purposes of the chase had come into Babylon as early as the time of Nabuchodonosor's reign ; the practice is, however, chiefly connected with Persia.) ' Now therefore, O king,' the courtiers go on to suggest, ' confirm the sentence and confirm the decree, that what is decreed by the Medes and Persians may not be altered, nor any man be allowed to transgress it.' That ' any man ' is, one feels, suggestive. But there are several points in the above quotation that deserve a moment's attention.

In the first place we must bear in mind that Darius was as much a stranger as Daniel to the Babylonian-born—in fact more so, because he had only recently come to live there while Daniel had been a Chaldean subject since his youth. He would therefore have taken it rather for granted that his native officials knew more about what was wanted in the country than he did. He was also under orders, remember, to adapt himself as far as possible to Babylonian ways.

---

[1] In the margin of the Authorised Version we read for this, ' came thronging to the king,' which in the Revised Version margin is rendered ' came tumultuously ' ; both these more vivid expressions suggest the pitch of animosity to which the ministers were keyed.

[2] Is this ' all ' meant to put the king off ? Is Darius being given to understand that Daniel's support has been previously obtained ?

He would therefore have been more than ready to fall in with any suggestion coming from his ministers. So it was that the piece of legislation in question did not receive the attention which its seriousness deserved. Here (Darius would have said to himself) was another paper to sign ; he had better do it now and get it over ; it was evidently something to do with religion so it couldn't matter much anyway. (Darius was a Mede.) If the document gave the king a second thought at all it was because of the clause which insisted that the promulgation should bear the official seal of the ' Medes and Persians.' The ministers had taken care to make this little detail perfectly clear : partly because of the fixed character which the names of these two nations lent to any enactment (the proverb has continued in the same form to the present day), and partly because the proposed statute was sufficiently Persian in feeling, that *should* Darius hesitate at all (and he was not likely to in view of the strong terms in which the petition had been couched) he would sign the thing out of fear of his Persian chief.[1]

The proclamation as we read it in the Bible text sounds like the kind of challenge that is pinned to the gate-house wall of a Hans Andersen castle. But for all the reference to ' lions ' and to the ' thirty days ' when there should be no god (save Cæsar), there was more to be said for the scheme at the time, and it is doubtful whether those who came under it ever regarded the decree as the mad caprice of a vain prince, which is what we would have expected them to think. This is just where the advising council were

[1] The specifically *Persian* character of the proposed apotheosis is a point which is hardly worth going into ; the reader is asked to accept it on faith that the Persians deified their heroes even more freely than did the hero-worshippers of surrounding nations.

so cunning : they played off the people on the king, and the king on the people. To the king the decree, as drafted by the representatives of the public, implied that since divine honours were paid to Egyptian, Assyrian, and Persian emperors it was now time that Babylon should arrange for some such fashionable deification. To the masses, on the other hand, the decree would be made to appear in quite different colours : Darius, behaving as well as he had done, deserved the kind of recognition which it was customary to give in other parts of the globe . . . and thirty days were after all only thirty days . . . the national gods would be admitted again, of course, and the public would probably find that devotion would receive an impetus, rather than a reverse, as a result of the suspension. . . .' Given under the seal of the Medes and Persians, all previous enactments notwithstanding '— which settled it.

We are not told how the man in the Babylonian street reacted to the new statute, but if he was at all like any other product of the industrial system he probably took it philosophically enough. In point of fact (to finish up this dull business) the adding on of one more name to the total of Babylon's deities— which is all that the whole affair would mean in thirty days' time—was probably not so upsetting to the average temple-goer as would have been a god's removal from the list (our knowledge of the previous reigns has shown us that). No, as long as there was —so to speak—no ' rebate,' pious Babylon might sleep in peace. And the thirty days, taken all in all, would probably be rather a relief.

ii

We can picture Daniel coming back from the tour of his territory, and ignorant of the events that have taken place in his absence. Not being a luxurious traveller his journeys are mostly conducted in a mule-drawn conveyance (something which is nearer to a cart than a carriage) which bumps and creaks and sways over the dusty road. The Prophet, placid and serene, has been sitting by the driver's side since early morning ; it is now past midday and they expect to reach Babylon by sunset. Daniel is pressing an open book to his lap and reads, with difficulty, the word of God. They rumble along past field after field of waving corn, gold in the glare of the afternoon sun ; an occasional streak of silver marks a canal. Daniel's presence, minister of state though the Prophet is, causes no excitement whatever in the mud-hut villages through which they pass : a few brown impudent children come out and stare, but that is all. As Babylon draws near the houses on the side of the road become less mean ; they have no longer the air, when grouped together, of being huddled up in the secrecy of whispered gossip ; they show through open doorways a floor of almost enamel blackness. We can think of Daniel taking all this in without very much detriment to his studies. One slender finger marks his place in the Hebrew text while his eyes are raised from time to time. The owners of the land through which he is travelling are mostly known to him ; he is one of that class ; he is one with them in everything except that which matters most. The gardens (we are nearing the outskirts) are a riot of colour ; even the blistering sun is powerless to fade the flowers that witness to the richness of the soil. Now, with the city walls in sight, there is more traffic on the road, and instead of an occasional group of fellow-travellers the Prophet meets every kind of vehicle and beast of burden.   There are merchants on errands of trade ;   there are covered caravans, mysterious and doubtless stuffy ;   there are ox-drawn wagons (piled up to an almost incredible height with foodstuffs, furniture, personal belongings, rugs, and finally—at the top—with family) . . . there are many-sized wheels and many-shaped hoofs to kick up the dust on the Babylon road.

Now Daniel has seen all this a hundred times before and, as we have suggested, it distracts him but little. One thing, however, *is* beginning to distract him (because he has not met it before without trouble ensuing) and that is the detachment of camel which is moving over the sky-line to join the road he is travelling. Daniel recognises the livery of the crown.   No, he is not arrested (why should he be ?), he is escorted merely.   Is this an honour or an insult ?   Unusual, whichever it is, but not (the Prophet reflects) unprecedented.   And, having folded up his tome, he looks at the riders who surround him, stern, silent, muscular exacters of the law ;   he looks at the beasts they ride, inscrutable also, supercilious in expression, indefatigable in endurance yet always tired-looking. What an amazing creature the camel is !   In a poem which is far too little known Major Kendall says of the camel that

> *His neck and legs are far too long ;*
> *He's clumsy, and he folds up wrong.*[1]

---

[1] He says further, in the same poem, that

> *Though devoid of outer grace,*
> *He wears a sneer upon his face.*

I have read somewhere that Mohammedans account for the know-

Once within the walls of Babylon the Prophet notices that the many little shrines and oratories which stand in every street are closed or boarded up, and that people no longer seem to be kneeling on their little mats in porches and doorways and in the courtyards of the temples. He asks one of his escort the meaning of this. Information is volunteered at once, and the Prophet (if he is on the alert at all) gets the impression that his response to the information is carefully noted by his informer.

> ' Now when Daniel knew this, that is to say that the law was made, he went into his house and, opening the windows in his upper chamber towards Jerusalem, he knelt down three times a day and adored and gave thanks before his God, as he had been accustomed to do before.'

With this verse in front of us it is not difficult to reconstruct the scene. He simply unloaded when he got home, and made straight for the roof of his house as usual : he was accustomed to pray there, and nothing in the world—barring physical force—would stop him ; his unpacking and his correspondence could wait till afterwards.

Daniel opened the long windows which led on to the flat roof, and there, kneeling half in and half out of his shelter (and framed consequently in the rectangle of

---

ing, superior look which the camel wears by saying that of the hundred names of God, they, the Mohammedans, are in possession of ninety-nine ; but that the camel knows the hundredth. Camels, lolloping over the sand, remind one of learned old gentlemen who have decided to exercise their limbs and have forgotten to stop. The impression has something to do with the mechanical energy of the legs as contrasted with the bored indifference (absent-mindedness even) of the face.

the opening) he turned his face towards Jerusalem.
It is admittedly no concern of ours to reconstruct the
Prophet's prayer as we have attempted to reconstruct
the setting of his Prophecy, but if we venture a suggestion in this respect we venture the suggestion that his
prayer was dry. It may be that his prayer was nothing
of the sort ; devotion may have come to him at once
and tears may have flowed as freely as the streams in the
king's park ; but if the prayer of the Prophet was
anything like the prayer of the saints who have come
after him, his thoughts up there on the housetop
were arid thoughts, disconnected thoughts, distracted
thoughts, or, more likely still, thoughts without shape
at all. (I shall come back to this in a minute.) We
see Daniel—as the spies doubtless saw him who were
posted on the roofs opposite—performing the various
ceremonies which he had learned as a boy in the
Temple. Thus had he prayed with his three Hebrew
friends sixty years ago ; thus also had he prayed
(recalling the words of Solomon : ' They shall pray to
Thee towards the way of the city which Thou hast
chosen, and towards the house which I have built to
Thy name ')[1] on his many journeys. Just as the
churches of the New Law face east, and as the martyrs
of Rome turned, in the arena, to their Bishop, God's
Vicar, so Daniel set his face towards the dwelling-place
of Jehovah—the Temple.

And so I imagine that at the end of an hour or so
(of what probably felt like a complete waste of time)
Daniel might have been seen to stumble to his feet in
the half-darkness, and make a move to go downstairs.
He sighs, probably, and frowns, and presses his lips
together, and accuses himself inwardly of being a lazy

[1] 3 Kings viii, 44.

man to have made his prayer so casually. The windows closed and the shutters lowered, he shuffles awkwardly over the bare boards, touching with the gentle feel of an old man the few familiar objects that lie between the window and the stair. ' I shall be here to-morrow, Lord, and again the day after ; grant only that I may make a better effort ; a miserable failure, this evening, was it not ? ' And then at the top of the stairs he gathers his copious garments around him, feels for the first drop, leans on the dusty rail, and makes his way slowly down to his room. Here there are people to be seen and letters to be read. It all seems, he tells himself, a desperate waste of time—especially when he might have been at the altar of God in Jerusalem all these years—but he supposes it will go on in this way until the end of his days. Well, he is serene : the last of those days will find him at it . . . if God should will it so . . . he, Daniel, is content.

NOTE

I have hesitated a long time before deciding to include the above paragraphs about the Prophet's prayer on the roof-top. As already allowed, nobody has the least reason for supposing the course of a prophet's prayer. I leave the above as it stands in the sole hope that for every ten whom it may annoy there may be one reader, or two, for whom it illustrates a consoling doctrine. Thus with all reverence and respect it seems worth while to hint—for the benefit of those whose prayer is dry and bitter and loveless—that possibly the prayer of the saints is much the same. We imagine that the experts in the spiritual life are more or less prayer-conscious all day long ; and that if we are to follow even remotely in their footsteps we should be able *at least in prayer time* to rise above distractions. We are only too conscious, however, that it is precisely during our set times for prayer that we do *not* rise above distractions : we are more at the mercy of silly thoughts *then* than at any other time of the day. Misconceptions would be avoided if we would only realise that however prayer-conscious the saints may be at other times it is with them (as with us) the set periods of recollection that are the least occupied (as a rule) with the thought of God. This is of course not a *universal* law—that prayer, as we think of it, escapes us every time we set ourselves to practise it—but it is a safe generalisation and can be borne out by countless examples from among the canonised and uncanonised servants of God. Men of prayer, when they are not on their knees, can teach people to pray, can work out methods of prayer, can compose set prayers, can even spend most of their working day *in* prayer (either in the habitual presence of God or in the practice of frequently repeated ejaculations), but when it comes to their hour of contemplation they can neither ' pray ' at the time nor give an account of it afterwards. ' Hopelessly distracted ' is the usual summing up, ' I couldn't tell you what I have been thinking about, but I'm fairly sure that it wasn't about God. The more seriously I try, the more laughable seems the result.'

It will be noticed that I have pictured Daniel as speaking to God when coming away from prayer. People are frequently puzzled to find that the moment their prayer is over they can speak to God quite easily. I suggest two reasons for this : first (the obvious one) that the soul, thinking it has failed dismally, tries to make up for lost time at the last minute (and *after* the last minute—out of its ' own time ' as it were) ; and second (the less obvious one—in fact this is a reason that is seldom explained to anxious souls who have made some effort in the practice of the spiritual life), that their prayer, which is deep and which they have not quite left off, is coming up again on to a level where it can be perceived by the senses. Their prayer has been too deep for them to see what has been going on—or even to know that there was anything going on at all. Consequently, in the process of returning to the normal (this is not to imply that there has been anything 'extraordinary' about the prayer—in the way of mystical graces and so forth—*or* that 'ordinary' people do not, normally, pray properly), a point is reached when the prayer is recognised *as* prayer. The prayer has been coming to the surface again. But obviously it is not such a good prayer *then* (i.e. at the point where it comes to be recognised) as it was when it was well below the surface. This is presumably what St Antony had in mind when he said that the best kind of prayer was to pray without knowing it. To suggest an example, it is like an electric fan after the current has been switched off : the machine goes on running for a little while, and as it slows down you begin to see the blades ; while the battery was connected you saw nothing, but it was *then* that the fan was doing the work.

In the same way people will claim that they can 'pray better' when they are walking up and down, or counting their ejaculations on a rosary, or repeating them to the rhythm of a clock or a steam-engine or what not. This again is almost always because such prayer is nearer to the surface, and so is never really lost sight of. As far as the senses go, yes, such prayer *does* feel much 'better.' But prayer is meant to go further than the senses : it is meant to go straight up to God Who is infinite while the senses are finite ; and in the process of approaching to God there is bound to be confusion of vision. For a soul to refuse to lose sight of its prayer is often to cramp the workings of grace : it is possible that the Holy Spirit is waiting to sink the prayer deeper into the soul, but is delayed by the state of mind which is met with on the way — the wanting to be sure that something is going on.

iii

In the meantime the agents of the anti-Daniel party have not been idle. The illegal gestures of devotion freely indulged in by the prominent Hebrew minister have been witnessed and written down as evidence ; it is a matter of a few moments to bring the information to the notice of the authorities.[1] But not on one single violation of the law, however open and defiant, would the Prophet be brought to book ; the promulgation of the decree had allowed a decent margin ; there must, if possible, be more than merely one instance of violation to cite. It might turn out, for example, that the Prophet had not read the law correctly, or that he had not been given time to adjust his liturgical life to meet the present need, or again, that he was really only praying for strength to put in practice the law which he was actually breaking. . . . No, the spies must return to their coigns of vantage and continue their watching for a few more days ; then would it be shown beyond all doubt that an official of the crown was setting at naught the laws which he was being paid to defend. ' Three times a day he maketh his prayer.'

iv

It is not likely that so succulent a piece of scandal and so fertile a source of speculation would have remained locked up in the narrow breast of the hired informer. The few days following the Prophet's home-

[1] We must bear in mind that Daniel's roof-top was not as lofty as some of the other, even more noble, roof-tops of the district, and that therefore what he did at the window of his ' upper chamber ' was more or less public property.

coming would have seen the arrival, at Daniel's house,
of Jews who had heard that their leader's actions were
being watched. A greater caution would be urged :
could the Prophet not perform his devotions at night
only ? and facing another way ? Would it not be
wise, perhaps, to use what remained of these ridiculous
' thirty days ' for visiting one or other of his more
distant farms ? Great solicitude would be shown for
Daniel's safety. Other callers, making no boast of dis-
interestedness whatever, would respectfully point out
the danger to which the Prophet's fellow-Jews (what
was left of them after the Return) were exposed :
could Daniel not conceal, as *they* had managed to
conceal, the worship which no believer would dream of
denying to the Lord ? Was not this indiscreet display
of piety on the Prophet's part just ever so slightly
thoughtless ? Was it even now too late for him to
follow in the train of those who were so nobly making
their way across the desert to the Holy Land ? Perhaps
the Lord in His Wisdom had ordained that this precise
situation should arise in order that His will might be
made clear, and that Daniel might be free to follow
his heart's desire. Had he not always longed to go with
the rest ? Here was God telling him, in the providential
guidance of circumstance, that the way was free. . . .

Daniel would doubtless have listened to whatever
suggestions were made. He would doubtless have
' discerned '[1] between what was prompted by fear for
his own safety and what was prompted by fear for the
safety of the prompters. But he would have held out
no hopes as regards changing his habitual practice.
He had not paraded his religion before, he would not

---

[1] As he had ' discerned ' between the meats of Nabuchodonosor's
table.

conceal it now ; his devotions were performed in the
sight of God, and if the men of Babylon had nothing
better to do than look at him, they were welcome. For
the enlightenment of those to whom he still seemed a
stumbling-block, Daniel would probably have gone on
more gently to explain that in the first place God's will
did not usually come by the way of threats from men,
and, in the second place, that it did not usually point
in the direction of flight. The Kingdom of heaven,
Daniel would have told his friends, was to be taken by
storm—not to be left because of one.

> ' Wherefore those men carefully watching him,
> found Daniel praying and making supplication to
> his God. And they came and spoke to the king
> concerning the edict : O king, hast thou not
> decreed that every man that should make a
> request to any of the gods, or men, but to thyself,
> O king, should be cast into the den of lions ? And
> the king answered them : The word is true.'

What an interview ! The ' carefully watching '
politicians standing before the king . . . pained expressions show clearly how distasteful it is to have to
report a fellow-nobleman ! But there is less respect,
notice, in their address than heretofore ; last time they
had to use all the weapons of diplomacy, this time they
are sure of themselves—and of Darius, and of Daniel.

' Then they answered and said : Daniel, who is of the
children of the Captivity, hath not regarded thy law
nor the decree that thou hast made ' (' thy ' law,
incidentally, ' the decree that thou hast made ') ' three
times a day he maketh his prayer.' Oh, they had a
very good case ; they could have convicted a hundred
Daniels on the evidence ; witnesses were falling over

one another. Now, then, was the law binding on all (they wanted to know), or was it not ? Yes, it was binding. In that case did the king know that one of his own cabinet ministers, Daniel ' of the Captivity ' (if you pleased) was slighting that law ? The king supposed he knew, but really he had not thought about it. Yes, now that he came to consider it, something (he supposed) would have to be done.

Darius, it must be insisted again, had regarded his measure as something which needed to be thrown to a restless and somewhat ' climbing ' people in order to keep them quiet. Darius had always kept both his eyes on Persia and only a foot in Babylon. True, it was the king's business to view the acts of council from every possible angle . . . well, he was to pay for his neglect : his friend was to be brought down by a fiction—a fiction which he, Darius, had made into a fact.

> ' Now when the king had heard these words he was very much grieved, and in behalf of Daniel he set himself to deliver him ; and even to sunset he laboured to save him.'

It looks as if Darius was a delightful man (quite different from Pilate to whom he has been frequently likened). Did he know, incidentally, that his Chaldean ministers were a pack of mountebanks ? Was he taken in by their silky manifestations of concern ? ' *So* unfortunate,' we can hear them say to their sovereign, ' one of our own colleagues too, and a personal friend of Your Majesty's . . . dear, dear, too bad . . . laws are laws, of course, Medes and Persians, you know . . . all very sad.' Oh yes, Darius *must* have seen through

N

it ! ' Even to sunset he laboured to save him,' but in vain : he had left no loophole in the law. . . .

v

It seems unlikely from the wording of the text that there was any kind of formal trial ; the procedure adopted for the occasion was probably carried out with some dispatch. The courtiers, with Daniel's previous record before them, would have realised the instant necessity of getting on with the matter. One assumes that Daniel, when next he gave himself to prayer, was simply arrested and packed off to some safe place to await the nightly feeding-time of lions. It is hardly probable that, after the sentence had once been passed, an interview took place between Daniel and the king : nothing could come of it.

> ' And they brought Daniel and cast him into the lions' den.'

If we are inclined to think of Daniel's march to the place of torture as a scene of high romance, winding up with a splendid *finale* as the Prophet says good-bye to all his friends, we are probably in error. The thing was a calculated persecution and not a pageant. It was not so much a popular spectacle as an unpopular expedient. That is one reason why it was rushed through in the inside of a day. In fact, far from being the kind of procession that was witnessed and taken part in by the masses, it is more than likely that no one was allowed to watch the respected foreigner as he walked to meet (what was expected to be) his death. Well within the palace enclosure the Prophet was led, a warder on either side of him, to that part of the establishment where the king's beasts were confined. Here he would have been met by the various officials whose presence was considered necessary to the occasion (a physician, the court chronicler, a representative from the temple, and perhaps one or two others[1]), and the party would have been joined a few minutes later by the king. It was dark (' till the going down of the sun ' had Darius laboured for a reprieve) so the proceedings would have been conducted by the light of pitch-torches or lanterns. There would have been the unfastening of locks and the drawing of bolts, and Daniel would have been hoisted on to the rail from which the lions' food was commonly pushed over into the pit.[2] Then there would have been the slow lowering of one of the greatest of the Prophets of Israel until the rope no longer held the strain. . . . From above, from where Darius was looking down into the pit, the slinking bodies of lions would have been seen to circle and counter-circle ; Darius would have noted the quick, determined stride which suggested that his lions were looking for something desperately important and that they did not want to be disturbed. ' Thy God,' calls out Darius in an agony, ' Whom thou servest always, He will deliver thee.' This verse of Holy Scripture is puzzling in the extreme. Did Darius really believe what he said ? Or was this merely an attempt to cheer the victim before the slaughter ? It would be gratifying to know

[1] We know that *some* of the accusers were present because we shall see them in a moment affixing their seals to the closed den, but there is no need to believe that the whole court were allowed to come and gloat.

[2] Pusey, in the lectures already referred to, goes into the question of the den (pp. 418–419), showing its probable construction and so forth, while Messrs Duff and Hope's book gives an illustration of the kind of cage which was in use, apparently, at this time.

that Darius was in good earnest—though he seems to have been asking a great deal of One to Whom he had as yet paid no heed. But we must not be hard on Darius, he will be bearing himself very creditably in a minute ; and besides, with the story of the ' Hebrew Children ' in his mind there is nothing to prevent him thinking : If flames, why not lions ?

There were a number of things which Daniel might have said in reply to the king's farewell salute, but time did not allow for repartee : there he was on the uneven floor . . . the clang of iron gates was ringing in his ears, his nostrils were filling with the reek of sweating hide and steaming dung. ' Into Thy hands, O Lord, do I commend my spirit. . . .'

vi

We have seen Daniel as an exile in Babylon in the early days ; we see him now within even narrower walls. He has surely learned by this time that to those who are free with the liberty of the children of God there is no such thing as exile. Or rather, all is exile—' for we have not here a lasting city, but we seek one that is to come '—and all is liberty—for we enjoy ' the freedom wherewith Christ hath made us free.' Daniel in Nabuchodonosor's palace and Daniel in Darius's lion-pit was equally able to live according to the pattern preordained for him by God ; therefore he was free. We are slaves only when we are unable to be what we are meant to be (when, for instance, we are not in a state of grace). Daniel was meant to be a saint, and he was able to practise sanctity as well in a dungeon as in a dining-room. ' Live in conformity to what you are and you will grow.' Isaias had managed to be Isaias within the narrow radius of his tree-trunk. He managed it so well that he is numbered among the martyr-saints of the Old Testament.

Man is hedged about with limitations : some are imposed by the natural order : some are forced upon him by his fellow-men ; some he subjects himself to from choice ; all are subject to God. Boundary-lines do not constitute captivity, they merely define the extent of freedom. ' Catholic Emancipation ' does not mean that until the year 1829 no post-Reformation Catholic was at liberty to lead a Catholic life, it merely means that after 1829 Catholics were enabled to live a fuller Catholic life. Daniel, in spite of the many crises in his career, was able at every stage to live a perfectly full Daniel-life. And because he did so he is ranked among the saints.

vii

We notice as we read the rest of the lions' den story in Holy Scripture that quite a lot of space is devoted to what was done outside the den, while there is comparatively little recorded of what went on within. Darius's thoughts are revealed, as we shall see, but never Daniel's. It is as if the incident is felt to owe its importance to the effect it had upon the king, rather than to the effect which it did *not* have upon the Prophet. This is perhaps explainable if what we have said about the Prophet's prayer in any way approaches the truth. But let us first take the text of Scripture, and, with the foregoing suggestion in mind, examine the events above ground before returning later to reconstruct (and account for) the happenings below.

' And a stone was brought and laid upon the mouth

of the den ; which the king sealed with his own ring and with the ring of his nobles,[1] that nothing should be done against Daniel. And the king went away to his house and laid himself down without taking supper ; and meat was not set before him, and even sleep departed from him. Then the king, rising very early in the morning, went in haste to the lions' den.' Here we can stop, reserving the next verses for the climax of the familiar story.

The little ceremony with the stone and the seals and the rings—taking place as it did the moment Daniel was out of the way—presents the curious and sinister mixture of the funeral and the conjuring-trick. No sooner is the body disposed of and the ropes rolled up, than an elaborate system of tapes and seals is embarked upon in order to ensure against deception. The reason for these precautions seems to have been double-edged : on the king's part to prevent the nobles from doing what the lions might leave undone, and on the nobles' part to make it impossible for the king to effect a rescue during the night. This extra-ordinary performance, enacted in the uncertain light of the flaming brands, shows that both parties entirely distrusted each other, but it reveals also the more unexpected fact that they equally distrusted the lions. There is something gloriously Gilbertian about the whole affair.

It is easy to see from the vivid account of the king's miserable evening and sleepless night where the writer derived his information. Being among the lions,

[1] A great number of these seals have come down to us from contemporary civilisation. Here there is definite mention of ' rings '; the more usual method was to roll a cylinder over damp clay. Darius Hystaspes is represented on one of these as engaged in a lion hunt.

Daniel would have been unable to follow the king's movements ; Darius, clearly, supplied the details himself. ('Couldn't think of dining,' Darius tells his friend afterwards, 'they wanted to give me my favourite dishes . . . not the slightest use. So I went to bed . . . not a wink of sleep the whole night. At about sunrise I came along to the den . . . but you know the rest. . . .') Darius had seen, earlier that same evening, the reflected light of fire in many pairs of eyes. No wonder he was unable to sleep. The lithe forms which he had seen pawing the walls of their pit were pulling at the curtains round his bed ; he was haunted by countless glowing points that shone at him as he lay waiting for the dawn.

But this is the climax of the story :

' Then the king, coming near to the den, cried with a lamentable voice to Daniel : Daniel, servant of the living God, hath thy God, thinkest thou, Whom thou servest always, been able, thinkest thou, to deliver thee from the lions ? And Daniel, answering the king, said : O king, live for ever . . .' and then he says how he has been spared. Imagine it ! The ' very early ' morning . . . the ' lamentable voice ' . . . the ringing salutation from the other side of the stone. . . . (One cannot help feeling that Darius's opening—when we consider that he had had the whole night to think it out—was neither a well turned nor a very profound remark.)

This night—whatever it has done for Daniel—has brought about a tremendous change in Darius : he believes in the Lord. How unforeseen is the result of yesterday's impeachment : the judge is bowing to the creed of the man whom he has condemned for holding it. Before ever the Prophet's voice is heard—and

whether the lions have done their grisly work or no—
Darius is a believer in Daniel's God. No sooner does
the convert make his profession of faith than the proof
of that faith is forthcoming. And Daniel, for his part,
hearing the ' lamentable,' still trembling ' Credo,' con-
gratulates the king on his witness to the Truth. It is
one of the most subtle situations in the whole of the
Old Testament.

' My God hath sent His Angel,' so runs the Prophet's
explanation of his safety, ' and hath shut up the
mouths of the lions, and they have not hurt me ; for-
asmuch as before Him justice hath been found in me ;
yea, and before thee, O king, I have done no offence.
Then was the king exceeding glad for him, and he commanded that Daniel should be taken out of the den ;
and Daniel was taken out of the den, and no hurt was
found in him because he believed in his God. And by
the king's commandment, those men were brought that
had accused Daniel, and they were cast into the lions'
den, they and their children and their wives, and they
did not reach the bottom of the den before the lions
caught them and broke all their bones in pieces.'

With this the more graphic aspect of the story, as
given in the Book of Daniel, closes ; it is here that our
Josephus adds a pretty detail of his own. According
to him a protest was lodged by the accusers on the plea
that Daniel had been offered to the lions too soon after
their previous meal, which meant that the experiment
had not been given a fair trial. Darius met the
objection (so Josephus) by providing the beasts with a
double portion each, and then only—when the animals
had eaten—introducing the nobles and their families
into the den.

(If the Josephus version is correct, then Darius, as

he peered over the rail for the second time in those few days, would have been able to reflect that it was certainly not repletion that had stayed the ferocity of his beasts before. What dear, faithful, obedient —not to say *discerning*—animals were these. . . . But too preoccupied were they just now to note their master's kindly look. Josephus is a poet! But to return :)

' Darius wrote to all the people, tribes, and languages, dwelling in the whole earth : Peace be multiplied unto you. It is decreed by me in all my empire and my kingdom [that] all men dread and fear the God of Daniel. For He is the living and eternal God for ever. He is the deliverer and saviour, doing signs and wonders in heaven and in earth ; Who hath delivered Daniel out of the lions' den. Now Daniel continued unto the reign of Darius and the reign of Cyrus the Persian.' With this the sixth chapter of Daniel closes (it is the last of the narrative chapters before the account of the Prophet's visions).

There can be no mistaking the import of Darius's final edict : his private conviction has ripened into a public proclamation. This, together with Nabuchodo- nosor's protestation of faith,[1] must have made interest- ing reading to the future archivists of Babylon. The God of Israel (say two of Babylon's noblest kings) is the One True God. Daniel's religion is Darius's religion —whatever Persia may say about it.

[1] To which we notice at once a quite remarkable resemblance. Did Daniel, I wonder, draw up the two documents ? He was cer- tainly entitled to do so, and would probably have been consulted in any case.

viii

Following the lead of Holy Scripture we have left
Daniel in his den and concerned ourselves with the
doings of others ; it is now that we must look for a
reason to justify the Prophet's reticence. The reason
I submit is not one to which I attach undue importance,
nor is it one which would find a place in any book
whose purpose was connected with Biblical criticism ;
it is merely the reason which seems to me the most
likely one. I am not above calling it a guess.

If Daniel is silent about his night of prayer among the
beasts, the reason may lie in the fact that he was praying. We have decided (subject to correction) that the
Prophet's spiritual state at this period was such that
it would have been almost impossible for him to give
an account of what went on in his prayer ; very good,
he prayed and gave no account—because he could not.
It might be argued in reply that this would be all
very well if we were considering his ordinary every-
day bell-to-bell period of meditation, but we are not ;
we are considering a night of prayer spent under very
unusual circumstances . . . would not the fact that
he was in danger of death have provided him with
material for a more particular prayer, ' affective '
prayer ? In answer it would have to be conceded that
any such calamity would, in the ordinary way, intensify
and—so to say—' focus ' a man's prayer. But then,
after the first two minutes Daniel was *not* in danger of
death. He would have realised very soon that what
had promised to be a martyrdom was in fact turning
out to be a rather dull evening. Thus his prayer, when
he gave himself to it (as he naturally would have done),
was nothing different from what it had been for the

last twenty years or more—an uninteresting, but not unrestful, blank.

But what, it will be urged, about the Angel ? Admittedly the Angel who came ' to shut up the mouths of the lions ' for him was a concrete manifestation of God's care which demanded definite acts of thanksgiving and so on. But the Angel (I answer) was only there for a little while, and then right at the beginning.

.   .   .   .   .

Daniel steps on to the grass of the king's lawn a free man. The dew is on his feet, and his clothes are red in the glow of the early morning sun. He is delighted about the conversion of his friend. For himself, he glories not at all ; there is bitter disappointment— humanly speaking—in his coming forth.[1] He has expected to be mauled to death for God, and now he is faced with resuming again his tasteless daily round of dry hard work . . . and prayer. This is not like the return of Nabuchodonosor, nor yet of Lazarus : it is much more like the return of the Curé of Ars when he thought he had escaped to pray and die . . . and was brought back to his parish to preach and live.

ix

' Daniel continued unto the reign of Darius, and the reign of Cyrus the Persian.' This is the end. No more is known of Daniel's closing years. What follows in his Book is, as we shall see, to be dovetailed in as best it can with what has gone before.

[1] Cf. ' Alas ! I found myself again on earth, and spiritual dryness once more took possession of my heart.' St Teresa of Lisieux, *Autobiography*, p. 213.

Is it fanciful to think that there is a hint to be got out of the abrupt conclusion ? If we like to read it so the final verse expresses a characteristic quality of Daniel's spiritual life. He ' continued on ' from reign to reign, always faithful, always serene. Primarily it is as a man of ' desires ' that the Prophet's name must be remembered. He longed for things all his life, some of which (very few) came about. That he *continued* so to desire, from the age of eighteen to (roughly) eighty-eight, is the miracle which, more than any other in his life, should win our admiration. Daniel continued for seventy years to desire a return to Juda ; he was disappointed. He desired to influence the masses on one point only ; he was disappointed. He was led to expect that his desire for a Messias would soon be realised ;[1] he was disappointed. If, as we have ventured to conjecture, his desires included martyrdom, he was, again, disappointed. If he lived long enough to see how those were behaving whom he had persuaded to go home to Jerusalem, he must have been—as they themselves were—disappointed.

Thus Daniel continues watching over his people, continues praying, continues working, continues hoping against hope, believing against belief, ' even unto the reign of Cyrus the Persian ' . . . and all he gets for it in this life is the word of the Lord telling him to ' go thy ways ur .il the time appointed . . . and stand in thy lot until the end of days.' ' Stand in thy lot '— there is the patience of the saints, there is faith.

---

[1] We judge as much from the revelation regarding the ' seventy weeks ' (ix, xii, *passim*).

CHAPTER XI

THE PROPHET DETECTING
(*Daniel xiv*, 1–21.)

i

'And Daniel was the king's guest and was honoured above all his friends.'

WHICH king was this? It can hardly have been Nabuchodonosor because the king here mentioned will be shown to have possessed nothing of Nabuchodonosor's astuteness; Nabuchodonosor, one feels, would have been quick to size up the quality of Bel's ministers; the sovereign who now appears before us (though entirely admirable in other ways as we shall see) was slow in this. Nabuchodonosor's son, Evil-Merodach, was notoriously wicked and so would hardly have been anxious either to further the cult of Bel or to ' convert ' the Hebrew Prophet ; nor would he have ' honoured Daniel above all his friends.' Nabonidus, though pious, was away from Babylon on archæological expeditions, most of the time ; also there is nothing to show that Daniel was a friend of his. Baltassar ignored Daniel throughout his period of power and therefore, as in the case of Evil-Merodach, cannot be said to have ' honoured him above his friends.' Darius was a Mede and so was not concerned with matters of Chaldean liturgy. Thus it narrows the choice to one of three names:

Neriglissar, second king upon the throne after Nabuchodonosor, Labashi-Marduk, who followed Neriglissar, and Cyrus whose reign overlapped Darius's coadjutorship. Of the first two possible claimants perhaps Neriglissar is the more likely ; Labashi-Marduk reigned only one year, which would scarcely give him time to get anxious about the continued cost of Bel's upkeep. With regard to Cyrus, it must be said that foremost among his champions is Driver, who, in the Introduction to his commentary, as good as assumes that if the Bel and dragon stories are true at all they belong to the reign of the Persian. It should be noted that Driver cites for this view the authority of Theodotion who gives the king's name in his emended Septuagint version (about which we shall have a word to say in a moment) ; he, Driver, also reminds us that Daniel lived on intimate terms with Cyrus who was therefore more likely than any other king before him to ' honour Daniel above all his friends.' This would seem to settle the matter. But for myself I still do not see why Cyrus, who was a Persian, should be so eager to serve Bel, who was a Babylonian. Nor, for the matter of that, can I see the great man Cyrus, any more than I can see the great man Nabuchodonosor, being twisted round the fingers of a band of clerical adventurers. But it is, all the same, no easy matter for me to get over the Theodotion text. What one would *like* to believe is that the king in this present episode is the king who appears in the one we have just been examining—in other words that he is Darius ; there is certainly traceable in the two accounts the same relationship between sovereign and subject. The only drawback to this identification is that we have to make a whole host of arbitrary assumptions ; first among which (contradicting our previous conclusions and postulating what we have denied to Driver) is the hypothesis that Darius was a worshipper of Babylon's idols. In the absence of evidence I shall refer to the man simply as 'the king' (while thinking of him as Darius nevertheless).

Thus it is seen that from now onwards the historical portions of this book will be becoming more and more conjectural ; there is however no commentator—at all events I have not come across him—who would dare to assign the incidents contained in Daniel's fourteenth chapter to any one reign or even decade of years. The Protestant Bible, as has been said, rejects ch. xiv altogether. The fact, however, that it has been accepted as canonical by the Church, and is contained in the Greek and Latin Bibles (though not in the Hebrew), puts, for Catholics, its authenticity as inspired Scripture beyond doubt.[1] The Septuagint text therefore— replaced in the Church by that of Theodotion—retains the Bel and dragon stories ;[2] though it must be added that they do not form part of Daniel's Book (they bear the bewildering title, ' From the Prophecy of Habacuc, son of Josue of the tribe of Levi ') ; the implication is that the chapter in question was to be found at one time or another in *some* Hebrew or Aramaic text, and that the source, happily translated into Greek, subsequently perished. Origen is all for keeping ch. xiv, and St Jerome appears to be in two minds about it. In any case, having it, it is high time we looked at it ; this introduction, though necessary, has been long enough.

[1] Appendix IV to Vol. III of the Westminster Version discusses (p. 254) the decisions of the Biblical Commission on this and similar points.
[2] See Pope, op. cit., pp. 377–380.

ii

' Now the Babylonians had an idol called Bel ; and there were spent upon him every day twelve great measures of fine flour, and forty sheep and six vessels of wine. And the king also worshipped him and went every day to adore him. But Daniel adored his God. And the king said to him : Why dost thou not adore Bel ? And he answered and said to him : Because I do not worship idols made with hands, but [I worship] the living God That created heaven and earth, and hath power over all flesh.'

The king evidently felt that Daniel was missing something ; Daniel evidently felt that the king was missing everything. Here was a god, argued the devout monarch, whose patronage was being dearly paid for by the nation ; the divine favour must be worth having; Daniel, a friend to the nation if ever there'd been one, must not be allowed to think himself excluded from the privileges of Babylon. . . . ' I do not worship idols,' is the answer to the invitation . . . and then : ' I worship the living God.'

' Doth not Bel seem to thee a *living god ?* Seest thou not how much he eateth and drinketh every day ? ' What an ingenuous remark ! Or was it, I wonder, the repetition of some slogan that had been circulated by the priests ? Had the king learnt up his *Answers to Objections*, and was he now—waving his hand, perhaps, at the cart-loads of food that were passing his window on their way to the temple—priding himself on having remembered the correct theological repartee. A god who ate heartily (so the Babylonians were doubtless told) was at least a living god, while one that fasted was not thereby proved spiritual. Daniel, recollect, had fasted from his youth.

> ' Then Daniel smiled and said : O king, be not deceived ; for this is but clay within and brass without, neither hath he eaten at any time.'

Anticipating the doctrine of the schoolmen, Daniel's attitude towards the miraculous was orthodoxy itself. He could afford to ' smile ' because he could afford to be reasonable ; he was able to bring sane reason against insane logic. The supernatural had always been more natural to him than the natural, but that was no reason why he should believe the unreasonable. He may have had no idea at this stage what was happening to the daily supply of provisions, but he knew quite well what was *not* happening to them : they were not being consumed by ' clay within and brass without.' Daniel would have had no difficulty in believing that the substance of bread and wine could change at the command of God, but what in actual fact he could *not* believe was that clay and brass should depend for nourishment upon bread and wine—and at the same time that clay and brass should call themselves a ' god.' God, it is true, asks for faith ; a faith that has some- times to transcend reason. But never a faith that flatly contradicts it. God is Truth. God pledges Himself to reason. Miracles were no difficulty to Daniel's faith—he had worked several himself—it was magic he could not accept. Nor was it that the idea of Bel's peculiar requirements was new to the Prophet ; he had seen much the same sort of thing among the countries which lay round about ; libations of wine and the slaying of beasts were expressions of true worship as well as of false ; he had assisted at the

o

Temple sacrifices as a boy. But there was all the difference in the world between slaying sheep on an altar and serving mutton on a dish; between wine that is poured out and wine that is poured in.

Now Daniel had been long enough in Babylon to know that the quantity of food now demanded by the Bel cultus was far in excess of what had seemed to satisfy in the past. There was something almost *too* human, Daniel would have reflected, about a variable appetite. A 'living' God, yes, but not more living than, say, twenty years ago.

> ' And the king being angry called for his priests and said to them : If you tell me not who it is that eateth these expenses, you shall die. But if you can show that Bel eateth these things, Daniel shall die, because he hath blasphemed against Bel. And Daniel said to the king : Be it done according to thy word.'

The king was angry, partly because his theological sally had spent itself and he did not know what the next 'answer to objections' was, and partly because he had ever such a slight suspicion that Daniel might possibly be right. One certain way of finding out, first, what the answer (if any) to the objection was, and second, whether there was anything in his suspicions after all, would be to send for the people most responsible for both the theory and the practice of the whole *affair* Bel. One suspects that he was angry also because Bel was becoming more expensive every day. He would know very soon if he was getting value for his money. (This king is alarmingly like Nabuchodonosor.)

The priests come in and stand before the king.

They are sleek and stout, and pasted all over with emblems of the god they serve (and who serves them) ; heaven knows they have every reason to parade the gratitude they owe him.   There follows the king's ultimatum, at the close of which one voice only is heard to make comment ; it is Daniel's voice. ' Be it done,' he says, 'according to thy word.' Surely the Prophet must have said this to annoy ? There was no call at that moment to make any observation whatever ; the others had preserved a respectful and entirely correct silence. The king had stated a fact, not laid a bet ; and ' be it *done*,' was Daniel's answer, ' according to thy word.' To the king the remark must have been exasperating as well as unseemly : the rumour would get about in the town that he had challenged the rival religions to a tournament. And here was Daniel—so sure of his God Who apparently cost him nothing in the way of revenue—standing in front of him with a smile on his face. . . .

' Now the priests of Bel were seventy besides their wives and little ones . . . and the king went with Daniel into the temple of Bel.' Let us join them there.

Much has been done of recent years to make the temple of Bel more prepossessing. The patronage and daily presence of the ruling sovereign have increased the popularity of Babylon's national deity. ' Vocations ' (as Daniel's *cicerone* would be eager to point out) have multiplied, and, with the admission of new subjects, money has flowed in. (Daniel would have noticed from the appearance of the subjects themselves that religious poverty was not a virtue for which they would have gone to the stake.) Architectural improvements have been carried out on a generous scale : the seating, flooring, roofing, windowing are as up to date as anything that Babylon can provide. But above all else it is the new sanctuary that claims the admiration of the visitor ; of this the clergy are particularly proud. It is ' holy ' (the guide explains) and so Daniel may not tread on it if he doesn't mind. . . .

Thus while the priest of Bel was at his patter and the king of Babylon was at his prayers, Daniel would have taken care to miss no detail. He would have seen the sacristans busy themselves with the preparations for the nightly feast (Bel ate only at night, behind closed doors) ; he would have watched the procession of neophytes as they bore the offerings up the aisle ; he would have seen these offerings, joints, sweets, fruits, and casks of wine, spread out before the great brass feet of Bel ; he would have seen the priests prostrate themselves in prayer ; he would have heard the blessing of the meats, the chanting of a hymn, the high-pitched note of the dismissal ; and then he would have seen the community file out in twos . . . so dignified, so calm.

Day after day, night after night, this farce had been repeated ; and though the Prophet had reason to smile at the whole proceeding he had reason to be somewhat saddened as well ; it was pathetic to think that devout souls were being duped by this kind of thing. The Prophet must have longed to bring these people to the truth ; both for their sake and for the sake of Truth Itself. He would have regarded the king's attitude as being representative : pious, credulous, and very much in earnest . . . fancying that that was a holocaust which in fact was nothing but a hoax. Babylon knew enough of God to ask that He should ' live ' ; the pity of it was that those who claimed to be His servants decided to use that knowledge for their own advantage. They brought their 'living god' so far down to earth that he must needs be lifted up again by wine. Satiety, not sacrifice, was what they had to offer.

'And the priests of Bel said : Behold we go out, and do thou, O king, set on the meats and make ready the wine and shut the door fast and seal it with thy own ring ; and when thou comest in the morning, if thou findest not that Bel hath eaten up all, we will suffer death, or else Daniel hath lied against us. And they little regarded it because they had made under the table a secret entrance, and they always came in by it, and consumed those things.'

Such were the priests of Bel.

They seemed so secure in their secret that the leader, speaking for the rest, could confidently strike the note of triumph : Daniel was already as good as beaten. They had gambled for years with the things which should have been sacred to them ; now they were playing for stakes which, though high, were for once perfectly lawful. The only mistake they made was in thinking they were perfectly safe. 'You see us going off to our quiet little houses,' says the high-priest, standing at the top of the temple steps in the gathering dusk, 'and the keys we leave with you. Arrange the table in whatever way you like ; make the door fast with the royal seal . . . and the proof of Bel shall be seen with the dawn.' A low bow sweeps gracefully down the line of seventy men, and the superior leads away his flock.

Inside the temple again, the king begins to lay out

the dishes ; Daniel, the ' unbeliever,' is not invited to
assist. So while the king (with his sleeves rolled up
and wearing that smile which is worn upon the faces
of those who are doing an unaccustomed act of service
which they know they will probably never have to do
again) is occupied on the sanctuary, Daniel is having
a quiet word with a squad of military that is waiting
in the porch ; these are the men who daily escort their
sovereign to and from the temple. Daniel, aware of
the fact that the members of the body-guard have
been chosen for their size and not for their creed (they
were probably Africans, and in any case ignorant of all
connected with either the king's or the Prophet's
religion) instructs them to collect for him the many
little braziers that are placed at intervals round the
walls. The coals have been left to burn low, and Daniel
is able to scrape together a pile of warm grey cinders.
This is the account in the Bible :

> ' They [the servants] brought ashes, and he
> [Daniel] sifted them all over the temple before the
> king ; and going forth they shut the door, and
> having sealed it with the king's ring, they
> departed.'

The king seems to have made no demur ; perhaps
he thought that the action indicated a yielding on
Daniel's part. (Could it be that Daniel was strewing
ashes—always the symbol of conversion and penance
—in lieu of the meats which he, the king, was privileged
to spread ?) The doors were sealed, the body-guard
was drawn up, the procession went home as usual to
the palace. One ventures to think that Daniel, the
while, was praying for the king, and that the king was
probably also praying for Daniel . . . and that the

priests, whose proper function it was to pray, were
praying for no one. The priests in all likelihood were
at the moment occupied in watching the return to the
palace : it would be an unfortunate thing (they would
have reflected as, peering between the slats of their
shutters, they counted the files that marched in the
street below) if a picket had been left in the temple.
. . . But it seems that the priests were satisfied that
as many returned to barracks as had come, for they

> ' went in by night according to their custom with
> their wives and with their children ; and they ate
> and drank up all.'

Thus when the king was parting from his chamberlains
for his nightly rest, the high-priest was joining with
his clergy for his nightly revel. There is nothing to
show that either sleep on the one hand, or entertainment on the other, suffered from the thought of what
awaited on the morrow.

> ' And the king rose early in the morning, and
> Daniel with him. And the king said : Are the
> seals whole, Daniel ? And he answered : They are
> whole, O king.'

The same kind of scene was to be repeated later on in
Daniel's life ; only then it would be the king alone
(Darius for certain this time) who would be the early
riser ; and Daniel, on that occasion, would be on the
other side of the seals.

Thus the king, with his friend striding beside him,
has arrived at the temple a good three hours before
his usual time ; the streets have been empty, and even
the priests who normally stand at the door to welcome

him have been forestalled ; the two men mount the steps alone. No artist, so far as I know, has made this scene the subject for a painting. I confess I am glad. Each can make his own picture for himself : the breeze playing in the silks of Daniel's and the king's clothes ; the sky becoming pinker every moment (and acquiring that dappled look which only a very early morning east of, say, Athens, seems willing to give to it— when the thousand little feathery clouds that are out of the way at other times give the impression of having been left behind by mistake in the hurried retreat of night) ; a faint mist softening the outlines of neighbouring walls ; dew sparkling on tufts of grass ; the two figures framed in the arch of a massive door . . . no, it would never do in paint.

' Are they whole, Daniel ? They are whole, O king.' The king was not asking for information—he had made quite sure that the great red blobs of wax were as they had been the night before—it was simply that he wanted Daniel to admit the obvious. Then followed the rending of seals and the breaking of tapes. (If Daniel was in the mood that he had been in when the experiment was mooted, he probably bent down and gathered up the fragments.) One somehow feels certain that it was the king, and not Daniel, who performed the ritual act of seal-breaking. Not only is it the proper function of the great to cut tapes, press all-important triggers, send up inaugural rockets and break bottles across the bows of ships, but here, in the case of the king in the Book of Daniel, the action was to be a personal demonstration. The magician on the stage will never allow another to whip away the handkerchief which reveals the empty (or, alternatively, the full) bowl. The king wanted to show to

Daniel, and to his own conscience, that the god of
Babylon 'lived.'

The key was turned, the huge door swung back on
its hinges, and the two men faced up the central aisle.
The sun had risen over the roofs behind them by now
and was shining through the open door full on the
raised sanctuary at the opposite end of the temple.

> ' And as soon as the king had opened the door
> he looked upon the table and cried out : Great
> art thou, O Bel, and there is not any deceit with
> thee. And Daniel laughed.'

Daniel's laugh, coming on top of the vindication of
all the king's hopes, must have been exceedingly
puzzling—not to say exasperating—to· the man who
was trying to enjoy the exquisite joy of relief. Daniel
had laughed. Either his chancellor was converted
(thought the king) or he was not. In neither case
should he have laughed.

> ' And he [Daniel] held the king that he should
> not go in, and he said : Behold the pavement, mark
> whose footsteps these are.'

The king ' beheld ' and ' marked,' for he said immediately, ' I see the footsteps of men and women and
children.'

Obviously this passage gives one of the most joyous
situations in Scripture. But there is something more
in it than what is merely superficially delightful.
The picture of the Hebrew Prophet with his arms
round the Babylonian's waist, preventing him from
further disturbing the ashes, is about as attractive

a view of Daniel as we would wish to have. But let us pass on from the purely picturesque to the partly pathetic ; let us look at the king for a moment, before looking back again at Daniel.

iii

I mean that the king, if he had not had Daniel there to help him, might have benefited nothing from the exposure of his false beliefs. The ground on which he had rested for years had been cut away from under him. Is it not possible that, with the sudden removal of one set of beliefs, he was tempted to do without another ? The supernatural had played him false : he despaired of the supernatural altogether. If this was his temptation—and I only put it forward as a possibility—then see how the circumstances surrounding it were almost in a conspiracy to hinder him in his crisis. The rays of the newly risen sun, warming his shoulders as he faced the evidence of his credulity, spoke to him of ' nature,' not of God. The great brass feet of Bel, polished and dazzling in the sunlight, were so obviously brass ; the litter of broken meats proclaimed a truth that was so obviously ' natural ' ; the temple architecture was so obviously more solid than anything for which it had stood. So that what with the sunshine, the sealing-wax, and the footprints in the cinders, there was every danger that the claims of the supernatural would be scattered to the winds. It is the same temptation which we have watched as it gained a hold on the materialist Nabuchodonosor, only this time the approach is from the other side. The king in the present story is tempted, once robbed of his ideals, to place his happiness in creatures ; the king in the other story places his happiness in creatures, and,

robbed of their possession, has nothing to fall back
upon until God gives him new ideals. ' What is the
good of making the act of faith,' says the king of the
Bel incident to himself, ' if this is what it brings you
to ? I shall know better in the future. Instead of
worrying about the spiritual life I shall be normal and
healthy and sane.' And yet I think we can say that
now, and only now, was the king mentally ready to
receive sound doctrine. What he needed to be told
(and what he doubtless *was* told, seeing that a Prophet
of the Lord was at his elbow) was that the material
things of God's creation were yet—for all their daylight, warmth, and sanity, for all their flaws and even
brazen imperfections—the work of the One True God.
The king needed to be told what the people of Athens
were told by St Paul ; that ' God Who made the
world, being Lord of heaven and earth, dwelleth not
in temples made with hands as though He wanted
anything,' as Bel evidently wanted things. ' We must
not suppose the Divinity to be like unto gold or silver
or stone, the graving of art and the device of man.'[1]

How much, one wonders, does the Daniel text leave
out ? Did the Prophet, who knew so much about the
Christ Who was to come,[2] explain to the king as the
two of them sat together in the porch waiting for the
arrival of the priests, that the time would come when
God would send into the world His only-begotten Son,
the LIVING GOD, and that in Him His creatures should
find life ? The Word would be made flesh, and would
dwell among us. Of Bel it had been claimed that he
possessed human attributes, but it had been insisted
also that he should dwell apart. . . . Did Daniel,

[1] Acts xvii, 24, 25, 29.
[2] Daniel ix and onwards. ' I insist that no other Prophet has
spoken so plainly of Christ,' says St Jerome.

speaking very gently to a monarch who was holding his head in his hands, show how *unreasonable* it was to cast aside the supernatural on the ground that the natural—and a very small percentage of it at that—was found to be unworthy of its kind ? Did he point out that Babylon had been fed upon mystery, and that mystery by itself was never meant to do the work of religion ? It was not always wise (Daniel may have suggested), and not always pleasing to God, to attribute to the Divinity anything that could not be made head or tail of here below.

Had Daniel lived about twenty-four centuries later (or, alternatively, had Chesterton lived about twenty-four centuries earlier) the Prophet could have quoted from a contemporary writer that ' real mystics don't hide mysteries, they reveal them. They set a thing up in broad daylight, and when you've seen it it's still a mystery. But the mystagogues hide a thing in darkness and secrecy, and when you find it, it's a platitude.' The priests of Bel had wrapped up their worship in ' darkness and secrecy,' with the result that when the sun shone upon their altars there was nothing to see but a platitude—and empty dishes.

iv

' And the king was angry.'

If crisis there was, the king came through it on the right side. His anger is the sign we have been looking for. How much more serious it would have been if the text had merely said that he was sad.

' Then he took the priests and their wives and their children. . . ' Imagine the excitement in the town ! Arrests were being made all the morning, and by noon half the houses in the neighbourhood of the temple

were untenanted. To us it seems hard on the children
that they should have been made to share the fate of
their parents ; the king doubtless saw the matter
from a different angle (' I have been paying for their
meals all this time, they must render the same account
as the rest ').

Before the story closes there is a strangely unexpected
detail which would not be found, one ventures to think,
in any other Sacred Book but that of Daniel. It
appears that after the arrest and before the execution
' they [the priests] showed him [the king] the private
doors by which they came in and consumed the things
that were on the table.' They rehearse for the king's
interest their manner of assembling for dinner ! The
words quoted reveal an unconcern for their fate and
a pride in their craft, which, if not exactly edifying, is
at least pleasing as a side-light on their spirit : for one
day at all events they were going to be perfectly
sincere. And they had only one day left to do it in.
Rather than feign a prayer to an earthly god who could
serve them no longer, they would play with the earthly
toys that had gained them their livelihood. Ropes
were pulled, bolts were shot, doors slid open on greased
runners, and the complicated mechanism of the sanctuary was demonstrated by a proud and perspiring
community in its shirt-sleeves to a bewildered king,
and to a Prophet who only wished that these unaccountable adventurers were better prepared to meet the
Lord.

' And the king therefore put them to death, and
delivered Bel into the power of Daniel, who destroyed
him and his temple.' *Vivida vis animi !* We may
rest assured that the work was strictly successful : Bel
occurs no more in the pages of Sacred Scripture.

CHAPTER XII

FURTHER EXPOSURES
(*Daniel xiv, 22–26.*)

WHEN we think of the number and variety of gods that were worshipped in Babylon during the century under consideration, it is perhaps no surprise to us when we learn that, as soon as Bel was disposed of, another and an even more ' living ' god took his place. It was a dragon. It is this word ' dragon ' that has lent a legendary character to the episode we are about to examine, but so true is the ring of every word in the brief account (which occupies six verses of text) that—apart altogether from the Church's *imprimatur* which settles the matter[1]—it is hard to see how the story can be questioned for a moment. As to when the incident took place it is again, as with the episode we have just been considering, impossible to say ; nor can we claim that the king of this is the king of the foregoing tale ; he certainly appears to be the same ; but if he was, he must have lapsed into much the same sort of errors that he had held before the Bel disclosures.

> ' And there was a great dragon in that place, and the Babylonians worshipped him.'

[1] Coming as it does from the same chapter of Daniel as the Bel incident, this story too, of course, is numbered among the deutero-canonical passages of the Bible. But it is no less inspired on that account.

For ' dragon,' then, let us read ' monster ' or ' beast '
throughout : the terminology of fable is ill-suited to
the bald recording of fact. I insist on referring to all
this as ' fact,' because people are far too ready to think
of this last chapter of Daniel as having no other purpose
than that of providing charming little tales for the
amusement of the young. We are dealing with the
inspired word of God, and though the word admits,
so to say, of variant spellings, it is a word which must
—from its root-origin—be true. These anecdotes in
the life of Daniel are quite definitely founded on fact ;
and for those (I do not number myself among them, I
may say) who find the ' dragon '-fact a stumbling-
block, the following suggestions may be submitted in
explanation of how such a thing as a beast-cultus
could possibly have taken hold of an otherwise
intelligent people.

Say a traveller from the remote south—from the
regions about the Red Sea, for example, where there are
crocodiles—has occasion to pass through Babylon ; as
a mark of appreciation he leaves a ' monster ' behind
him when he goes (say it is a specimen of some amphi-
bious animal as yet unknown to the zoology of
Chaldea) ; should the gift, moreover, be made to one
or other of the gods or to the priests, then there is all
the more reason for the mystery which would surround
the monster's origins : the donor has preferred to
remain anonymous. No unofficial person has the least
idea that the animal is in the town. The traveller,
who is the only man who can explain where it came
from (and what it is), goes on with his journey. Now,
and not till now, is the new ' living god ' exposed for
public veneration. Kept at a discreet distance from
the devout and curious, the beast looks most impressive

against a background of cyprus and acacia trees. The monster readily wins its way to the favour which has lately been extended to—and then by popular consent wrested from—its predecessor, Bel.[1]

In any case, whatever the animal's past history, the men who are now responsible for promoting its cult have learned a lesson from past experiments of the same kind. Thus if it is still a living god that Babylonians are asking for, then a living god they shall have; but this time there will be no mistake about the manner in which it keeps body and soul together—it would do so openly : the oblations of its votaries would be *seen* disappearing. As a candle put up before a shrine, so a dove would be put down before the beast . . . and would be seen consumed.

And so in the cool of the evening devout Babylon would file out to that part of the royal grounds which had been turned into a centre of pilgrimage.[2] Open-air worship would have been voted far more satisfactory than praying in a temple : not only was there less scope for clerical fraud (though the present deity was clearly superior to Bel, and superior, too, to any tests which might be applied by a Prophet of Israel), but also you got more out of it : you prayed, you were entertained, you were in healthy surroundings, you were given proof of your belief . . . there was much to be said for religion after all.

In due course Daniel received an order from the king.

[1] It has been represented to me that no animal known to man could possibly look at all like a dragon. But take a crocodile or a turtle, and add to it a pair of wings (the deity-mongers of Babylon were not above adding wings as they had added attributes to their gods), and some paint, and you get, with a skilful use of reflected light, what I should think would be a very convincing dragon.

[2] A portion of the hanging-gardens may even have been railed off to accommodate the divinity.

'And the king said to Daniel: Behold thou canst not say now that this is not a living god. Adore him therefore.' The peremptory tone of the command suggests a more forceful person than Darius, but it is still difficult to believe that Cyrus or Nabuchodonosor could have been taken in by the appearance of the monster—however monstrous.

'And Daniel said: I adore the Lord my God, for He is a living God. But that is no living god.' The stinging contempt of the Prophet's words! The form of the reply seems to imply that the interview took place in the presence of the animal, Daniel nodding in its direction at the word 'that.' 'But give me leave, O king,' the Prophet went on, 'and I will kill this dragon without sword or club. And the king said: I give thee leave.'

Clearly the same pen is at work on this as on the preceding story; the writer evidently loves the crisp dialogue of unloquacious men who hold opposite views. Clipped and economical, it is the same language of challenge with which we have grown familiar from Nabuchodonosor and Baltassar days. The Book of Daniel is all of one piece. But this time it is Daniel who lays the bet, and it is the king who takes it up. The king's 'I give thee leave' admirably balances the 'Be it done, O king' from the story that has gone before.

Notice further the tempering of the Prophet's weapons according to the evil which he has to fight. His aim here is to make the animal, and therefore the cult with its adherents, look ridiculous. We shall see him in a minute choosing a ridiculous weapon to do it with. Throughout his whole career Daniel is consistency itself: he had set about the correcting of

P

Nabuchodonosor's errors by an appeal to the man's
reason (because he judged that Nabuchodonosor had
one), putting before him the Power and the Providence
of God ; he had disabused Baltassar of false belief by
implanting in him the idea of Fear ; he had led Darius
to embrace the true religion (or at all events to acknow-
ledge the God of Israel) by prayer, by example, and
finally by miracle ; he had overthrown Bel by a piece
of straightforward detection, revealing the plan not as
he would have revealed a dream, but rather as he would
have exposed a crime. The Prophet not only rises to
every occasion with the appropriate answer to the
difficulty, but he does so in the language of his anta-
gonists. The idea of paying supernatural respect to
something which divided its time between basking in
the sun and floating in a pool was *so* preposterous that
good honest derision was the means best suited to the
apologetics of the moment.

> ' Then Daniel took pitch and fat and hair, and
> boiled them together ; and he made lumps, and
> put them into the dragon's mouth ; and the dragon
> burst asunder. And he said : Behold him whom
> you worshipped.'

With his mystified domestics we can watch the man
of God among the saucepans. The steam is bringing
the colour to his cheeks and he is singing the psalms
of David as he works. We can watch him, too, as he
drives through the city to the shrine. A tray, covered
with a spotless linen cloth, is on his lap, and he passes
along Nabuchodonosor's Processional Way as one who
is going to a tourney ; but it will be more than a
tourney, it will be a triumph. Arrived at the shrine
(which is at the same time a cage) there is the pushing

of dark, soggy cakes between brass bars and into waiting jaws. There are the silent spectators; there is the not unpleasant sound of persistent chewing . . . more cakes . . . the chewing ceases . . . and then, some hours later, there is the passing of the poor, over-honoured, over-nourished beast . . .

'Behold him whom you worshipped.' The last word is in the past tense: Babylon has already withdrawn its favour.

.   .   .   .   .

The gardens that had enjoyed the brief privilege of Olympus have reverted to their former status. Night has come down to shroud an empty garden temple in a blessed peace. Greater care than ever will be taken now that the animals which wander over the well-tended lawns will wander unmolested. And Daniel, as he makes his way home in the moonlight, is doubtless preparing his soul for the storm which he knows must surely break. Soon we shall see him caught up once more in the tempest of jealousy and anti-Jewish hate; to-night at least let us leave him in the peaceful enjoyment of the things of God. The light of the moon falls like silver rain on an ornamental pool that has but lately lapped a 'god.' Daniel retires to rest, feeling (one hopes) that his day has not been altogether wasted.

CHAPTER XIII

DANIEL AGAIN WITH THE LIONS
(*Daniel xiv, 27–42.*)

i

FOLLOWING close upon the heels of the dragon story—so close that it would seem to be a continuation of it (which it almost certainly is not)—comes the last recorded incident in the Book of Daniel. Again the same difficulty about the date; again the same difficulty about the king. The only suggestion which in this connexion I am prepared to make is that the king in the lion story before us is not the king (Darius) of the lion story with which we have already dealt; that is to say the present account of the Prophet's arrest and subsequent consignment to the den is not an elaboration, merely, of the facts which appear in Daniel's ch. vi; it is a different episode altogether, taking place (almost certainly) before the other, and for quite different reasons; taking place at the instance, moreover, of quite a different class of person. This time the sentence is not passed and carried out because a few Chaldean noblemen are feeling in a spiteful mood; certain it is that jealousy was at the back of both agitations, but in the case before us it is a jealousy of Juda's growing power in Babylon; it is more now a question of national *malaise* finding expression in anti-Jewish outcry ; it is not so much a private persecution as a pogrom.

Let us examine what actually happened, and had been happening, before the shout was raised that Daniel must be done away with.

The people of Babylon were in a difficult position theologically. Their faith in Bel had been destroyed because he could not justify openly what had been claimed for him : he could not eat in public. A god was then raised whose sole right to men's homage rested on the fact that he *could* eat in public. So when it was discovered that there were some things which even *he* could not eat—in public or in private—the people of Babylon did not know what to believe in. Were *none* of their gods able to vindicate themselves ? No ? In that case, they, the men of Babylon, would do the vindicating for them.

Thus it came about that the Chaldean mob, not knowing where to turn, did what many mobs have, in the like predicament, done since : they turned against the Jews.

' They [the men of Babylon] took great indignation, and, being gathered together against the king, they said : The king is become a Jew . . . deliver to us Daniel or else we will destroy thee and thy house.' How very reminiscent is this of another crowd, another threat, another ruler, and another Scapegoat.

The Jews, always and everywhere a suspect race (but more so in Babylon to which they had come as captives and stayed as capitalists), were represented to the king as being those responsible for the chaotic state of religion in the country. He was told, and told bluntly, that a rumour of his ' conversion ' was abroad ; if this were, in the event, to take place, then the very roots of a time-honoured system of worship would be cut away from under Babylon's faith. At any cost the king must be given cause to steady his religious vacillations. Daniel the Jew chancellor (for it was he who was at the bottom of it all) must go. In the name of the national religion he must be delivered up . . . failing which, 'we will destroy thee and thy house.'

It was in the name of religion, then, that Daniel's life was forfeit. His accusers could not say he was an 'illuminate,' a 'visionary' (and on that account an unsafe person to have about the court), because in the capacity of seer he had proved himself to several of their own kings beyond all possible doubt ; in fact he had been requisitioned, when native prophets had shown themselves to have been utterly useless, for that very purpose. Again it was not as a materialist, as one who denied the unseen, that he could be condemned : he frankly professed the Unseen. It was precisely because *too much* of Bel and *too much* of the beast had been paraded before the eyes of men that Daniel had exposed the all-important little that was hid. Daniel would have been the first to admit, with his predecessor Isaias, that God was a 'hidden God indeed,' but he would have denied at the same time the right of man to hide Him.

Unable, then, to choose between charging Judaism with incredulity on the one hand and gullibility on the other, the leaders of the disturbance decided to get the Prophet convicted for 'disturbing the existing order of things.' Clearly this would meet the case. No attention need be drawn to the question of how far the 'order of things' still existed now that Daniel had disturbed them ; the thing to be aimed at was to get Daniel out of the way ; suppressive

measures against the Jews as a class would follow
later on.

' It is expedient that one man should die ' (so it was
argued of the Lord Whom Daniel heralded) ' that the
whole nation perish not.'[1] How does this compare
with ' Deliver us, Daniel, or we will destroy thee and
thy house ' ? ' If thou release this Man, thou art not
Cæsar's friend,'[2] was the threat which finally decided
Pilate's mind. It is impossible to say how far Daniel
was granted to see into the sufferings of Our Lord ;
the most that appears in his pages is the prophecy that
' He shall be slain, and the people that deny Him shall
not be His ' (and these words are thought to have
been said years later when the present crisis had
passed) ; but however much or however little the
Prophet knew about the Passion there is something
very striking about the parallel which it bears to his
own. ' And so Pilate being willing to satisfy the
people, released to them Barabbas and delivered up
Jesus,' is the text of St Mark.[3] ' And the king saw that
they pressed upon him violently, and being constrained
by necessity, he delivered Daniel to them,' is the text
of Daniel.

And even if the Prophet had not an inkling of the
manner in which his Messias was to die, he had at least
the older Scriptures before him to show the way in
which the just should suffer persecution. The Book of
Wisdom would have warned him of the kind of thing
he was to expect : ' Let our strength be in the law of
justice,' say those who find fault with the saints—it is
usually in the name of justice that the just are done
to death, ' Let us therefore lie in wait for the just

[1] John xi, 50. [2] John xix, 12.
[3] Mark xv, 15.

because he is not for our turn ; and he is contrary to
our doings and he upbraideth us and divulgeth against
us our sins . . . he is grievous to us even to behold '
—Daniel's features would have differed from the
Babylonian type—' his life is not like other men's, and
his ways are very different . . . let us examine him by
tortures that we may know his meekness and try his
patience.'[1]

So to return to the text which immediately concerns
us :

> ' They cast him into the den of lions and he was
> there six days ; and in the den were seven lions,
> and they had given to them two carcasses every
> day and two sheep ; but then they [the daily
> provisions] were not given to them that they
> might devour Daniel.'

Thus to Daniel also, as well as to Christ, were
Isaias's words appropriate : ' He hath borne the sins
of many and hath prayed for the transgressors.' Daniel
went down into the pit, praying for the vindication of
the Lord of Israel before the men of Babylon, himself
glad to be ' a testimony to them and to the gentiles.'[2]

We can leave the Prophet with the lions while we
look in another direction altogether—towards Judea.

ii

' Now there was in Judea a prophet called Habacuc ;
and he had boiled potage and had broken bread in a
bowl, and was going into the field to carry it to the
reapers. And the Angel of the Lord said to Habacuc :

---

[1] Wisdom ii, 11–22.   [2] Cf. Matthew x, 18.

Carry the dinner which thou hast into Babylon to Daniel who is in the lions' den.' The vivid picture has obviously been painted for Daniel's benefit by the man who had actually boiled the potage and broken the bread ; Habacuc, during the solitary meal which followed, must have repeated the circumstances of his sudden summons.

> ' And Habacuc said : Lord, I never saw Baby-
> lon, nor do I know the den.'

If the Habacuc of this incident is (as I think him to be) the Minor Prophet of that name, then there is all the more reason why he should loathe the idea of being sent to Babylon : he had preached against the place in early life. But even if he was not the writer of the Prophecy, his reluctance to undertake the mission is understandable enough. There are many souls who frame for themselves a system of serving God, and who, when once the order of the system is interfered with, are incapable of seeing a new form of service in the newly signified will of God. Habacuc was one of these. His system was an excellent one ; it involved charity shown to hungry reapers ; it was both inspired and blessed by God. On a particular day the work of preparation was interrupted, and the prophet was told to apply his charity in a different direction. So used was Habacuc to his way of working for God that He for Whom the Work was being done was not immediately seen in the object to which the act of charity was now directed. Habacuc was wedded to his work : he was mistaking a means for the end.

But God, fortunately, did not listen to Habacuc's excuses ; nor did He reprove him for his want of confidence ; He simply took the matter into His own

hands and bent the prophet's will to meet His own.
' And the Angel of the Lord took him by the top of
his head, and set him in Babylon over the den by the
force of His spirit.'

Habacuc was a good man, and the Lord had regard
to his patient, not-very-exciting labour. That Habacuc
had been slow to respond to a sudden grace was not
referred to again. (We note in passing how careful
is God to spare the blushes of those who fail Him . . .
be it those who fail Him ever so little—like Habacuc
or Heli—or those who fail Him ever so much—like
St Peter or even Judas. Nowhere does God expose
the infidelity. God is the last to expose the un-
generosity of man. The Betrayal was made known
by Judas, not by Jesus. Mary Magdalen, Augustine,
Margaret of Cortona—all the penitents of history—
have been responsible for the publicity of their sin.
In the court of sanctity the ordinary order is reversed :
the prisoner first pleads guilty, and then, when the trial
has run its course, is acquitted !)

Once arrived at the den of lions, ' Habacuc cried,
saying : O Daniel, thou servant of God, take the
dinner that God hath sent thee. And Daniel said :
Thou hast remembered me, O God, and Thou hast
not forsaken them that love Thee.'

So Habacuc has risen to the occasion : no word to
Daniel about his dislike of Babylon, not a hint to show
that he is not fond of lions.

' And Daniel arose and ate.' Not a word, apparently,
did Daniel address to Habacuc. He praised the Lord,
said grace, and began his meal.

     ' And the Angel of the Lord presently set
Habacuc again in his own place.'

    .   .   .   .   .

Habacuc is back again in Judea. He is sitting on the hard mud floor of his kitchen, wondering if the whole incident has been a dream and not a reality at all. . . . Ah, the empty plates are evidence of his ' experience ' : he will show them to the reapers when he tells of the cause of his delay. But he will never be believed ; the reapers will accuse him of being idle ; or greedy. Habacuc begins to cook another potage ; he breaks more bread. . . . In half an hour he is shuffling across the fields with his steaming burden. In an hour he is back again—in his oratory this time —and going over and over in his mind the (humanly) unaccountable nature of this afternoon's happenings.

.   .   .   .   .

' Upon the seventh day the king came to bewail Daniel ; and he came to the den and looked in, and behold Daniel was sitting in the midst of the lions.'

The meal which Habacuc had brought him must, like that which had been put before Elias under the juniper tree,[1] have been possessed of nourishing properties quite above the ordinary ; seven whole days had Daniel been without naturally procured food by the time that he was relieved by the king's visit (the lions, too, had been fasting all this time).

' And the king cried out with a loud voice saying : Great art thou, O Lord the God of Daniel. And he drew him out of the lions' den.'

Handsome as the king's acknowledgement is, there is nothing like the same burst of generosity about this protestation as there was (or rather, if we consider the

[1] 3 Kings xix, 8.

thing chronologically, as there ' will be ') about Darius's attitude towards the Prophet and towards the Prophet's faith. There is, of course, a marked similarity in the two events. For one thing there is the curious feeling with regard to both accounts that the whole business is rather in the nature of a speculation : ' we-shall-see-in-the-morning-who's-won ' is the key-note of ch. vi and Ch. XIV alike (only, of course, in the present story the result of the experiment is only disclosed on the seventh morning, not the first). It is, perhaps, this strike-a-bargain aspect of both incidents that inclines us to treat the narrative portions of Daniel too light-heartedly ; if we have ourselves erred in this respect we are sorry (though our Apologia will be found in the concluding chapter).

Notice that in this present record there is none of the warmth of feeling which distinguished the former ; the king who was able quite comfortably to sleep through seven nights on end before he ' bewailed ' is not treated as largely by the writer as was Darius, who could not bear to sit the one night through. There is here no mention of the ' lamentable voice,' nor does the king recount the details of his disquiet. The text in front of us, moreover, suggests far more forcibly than the other that the king was not expecting to find a trace of Daniel : ' he came to the den and looked in, and behold, Daniel was sitting in the midst,' etc., that ' behold,' to my mind, gives the king away. But, like the other unbelieving monarchs of Babylon before him, he declared his admiration for the God of Israel, admitting, after what must have been some rapid thinking, that ' great was He, the God of Daniel.' He had not been ready to admit as much an hour ago. In Darius's case the act of faith was *followed* by the proof ; in this it is the proof which elicits the act of faith. Never mind, the king was as good as his word : he witnessed—albeit in the somewhat barbarous fashion of his time—to the ' greatness ' of the God he had confessed :

' But those who had been the cause of his [Daniel's] destruction, he [the king] cast into the den, and they were devoured in a moment before him '—which must have pleased Josephus when he came to the passage— ' then he said : Let all the inhabitants of the whole earth fear the God of Daniel, for He is the Saviour working signs and wonders in the earth, Who hath delivered Daniel out of the lions' den.' These are the last words in the Book of Daniel.

iii

No less than four crowned heads have now bowed to the name of the One True God. Seeing, too, that some of the necks have been singularly stiff, one wonders how the Prophet dealt with the inevitable sense of personal triumph. Not that Daniel was in much danger of becoming a snob (though snobbishness must ever be a trap for the unofficial court-confessor —which is more or less what Daniel was) ; it was rather that the sight of his work among the un-believing obstinate was likely to prove a consoling vision when balanced up against his work among the believing lethargic. Such consoling visions are not to be rested in by the selfless workers for God's glory ; nor, for the matter of that, are the discouraging visions to be taken too seriously either. Where Daniel suc-ceeded and where Daniel failed it was not for the Prophet to pronounce. Nor, as a fact, did he.

But before we close the chapter which describes the fourth royal conversion, we must note in passing how violent the converts have been in the expressions of their new-found belief. Once they were on the right side of the line there was not only no going back, but there was provided strong incentive for everyone else going forward. And in the cases of the Bel incident, the two lion stories, and probably where the ' monster ' was concerned, those who had deliberately placed themselves on the wrong side of the line were done away with altogether. Without such a backing as the rest of Scripture affords, the Book of Daniel might, in this connexion, give a somewhat unusual view of the value of human life. But *if* life appears here as something of a game, it is certainly as a game which is of the highest importance : *so* important is the issue felt to be that the necessity of removing out of hand the people who cheat is found to be the only possible way of conducting it.[1]

Ending thus on a note of triumph which is all the more triumphant because resounding to the glory of God and not to the glory of Daniel, the finishing strophes of the Prophet's song are found to be nothing different in effect from all that has gone before : the victories of Daniel have been the victories of the Lord. Since the time when, in Nabuchodonosor's reign, the Lord had given to Daniel ' the understanding also of visions and dreams,' right on until the end of the Prophet's long life, that ' understanding ' was ever being referred back again to God. It was the Lord Who had read, through Daniel's eyes, the writing on

[1] A lively interest is added to the game by reason of the fact that those players who decide, in spite of everything, to risk it *and* cheat, thereby seem to commit themselves to a policy of fastening the accusation of foul play upon everybody else.

Baltassar's wall; it was the Lord Who had told the world, through Daniel's lips, of the Christ Who was to come; it was the Lord Who had rescued Susanna, overthrown Bel, emptied the garden-temple of its god, delivered the Hebrew children from the fiery furnace, and stopped the mouths of lions in two separate dens. God had been the Prophet's victory and his strength.

'Thou hast remembered me, O God, and Thou hast not forsaken them that love Thee.' Such was Daniel's thanksgiving prayer in the presence of the prophet Habacuc. No, God had not 'forsaken' His servant, and His servant had not ceased to 'love.' And if we ask further the occasion of this 'remembering' on the part of God, and if we ask also when, on Daniel's part, this 'loving' first revealed itself, the answer to both our questions lies (I think) in a single passage from an earlier page. There was a day when the Prophet had 'stood trembling in his consternation' (he tells us about it in the apocalyptic section which I am afraid I have left out), and the testimony which was granted to him on that occasion is an answer to our speculations as to when the work of grace in Daniel's soul may be said to have—in an *especial* way—begun. 'From the day that thou didst set thy heart to afflict thyself in the sight of God,' the Prophet is told, 'thy words have been heard; and I am come for thy words.'[1] It was penance, then, which had set in motion the whole train of graces, the course of which we have been following. Perhaps we have guessed as much already. In that case we have nothing more to learn of Daniel: we have understood the fullness of the Prophet's burden. But for those who have hitherto made Daniel's proper virtue twofold merely—his

[1] x, 12.

'continuing faithful' and his invincible 'desire'—
there can be added, on this the last page of the man's
life, a third determining quality to his spirit : the
'afflicting' of himself 'in the sight of his God.' It was
this penance that drew to Daniel the attention of his
Lord ; from the very 'first day' of his ascetical life,
Daniel's prayers 'have been heard . . . and I am come
for thy words.' *Our* words, therefore, and *our* desires,
must surely stand a better chance of being listened to
when salted with the self-affliction of the saints. Else
shall we not blush to hear the Voice which Daniel
heard, 'I am come . . . for thy words' ?

CHAPTER XIV

CONCLUSION

i

DANIEL'S feast is kept in the Roman Martyrology on July 1st. Though it is as a Prophet that his sanctity has been preserved for us, it is interesting to notice that nowhere in the Old Testament is that title expressly attributed to Daniel; he himself never claims to be a ' prophet,' and Ezechiel (who is responsible more than any other for promoting veneration to Daniel's name) speaks only of his ' righteousness ' and supernatural ' wisdom.'[1]

' Later Jewish writings,' says Driver,[2] ' contain various anecdotes relating to Daniel; but they are destitute of historical value '; Driver further cites Farrar for such accounts as have come down to us of Daniel's ' opposition to idolatry, and of his good deeds.'

There appears to be a tradition that Daniel returned to Judea and that he died there. Another and a stronger tradition (and one which bears out the statement of the Martyrology that Babylon was the scene of Daniel's death) asserts that the Prophet was buried in Chaldea; in keeping with this is the Arab legend which discovers the sacred remains, in the seventh

---

[1] Ezechiel xiv, 14, 20 ; xxviii, 3.
[2] Op. cit., Introduction, xxi.

century A.D., at Susa in Chaldea ; the same legend
goes on to say that King Sangar transferred the body
(in a glass coffin) from the place where it had lain
hidden for so long to a still more secret resting-
place at the bottom of the River Shaour. It
appears that Benjamin of Tudela, when he visited
Susa in 1160, found Daniel's shrine the centre of
veneration. Seven thousand Jews inhabited the place ;
fourteen synagogues could be counted in the vicinity.
But though the tomb was visible and received these
honours, the exact locality of the bones was never
known. They may be, still, somewhere in the river
bed. 'What purports to be the tomb of Daniel,'
says Driver (who gives a sad-looking illustration of it
as the frontispiece of his book), ' is shown to the
present day, a little west of the mounds which mark
the site of the ancient acropolis of Susa, on the opposite
side of the Shaour.'

ii

We have come almost to the end of this book and
nothing has yet been said of the manner in which Daniel
received the name ' man of desires ' with which we have
ventured to label him on the cover.[1] The whole thing
can be told in a paragraph ; all three citations are
from the prophetical portion of the Prophet's writings.

The first occasion was when, during his prayer,
' the Angel ' flew to Daniel and explained to him the
meaning of the ' seventy weeks.' It is a delightful

[1] See note. p. 7 ; other versions than ours have ' greatly beloved '
instead of ' man of desires ' ; the Latin in our version is simply ' vir
desideriorum.'

passage (ix, 22) in which we hear the Prophet 'confessing his sin and the sin of his people Israel, and presenting his supplication before the Lord.' In the chapter following we read of Daniel 'in a deep sleep' on the twenty-fourth day of Nisan; he has just been granted a vision the force of which has quite overwhelmed him; he is raised to his feet by one who calls him a 'man of desires.' It is not perfectly certain who this is who was 'sent' to encourage Daniel; at all events the voice represents the voice of God. On the third occasion (also from ch. x) the same mysterious and luminous being appears again (he is 'one like the appearance of a man') and, as previously, restores strength to the Prophet's swooning body: 'Fear not, O man of desires, peace be to thee, take courage and be strong. And when he spoke to me I grew strong. . . .' The passage is an illuminating one: it shows that Daniel, like every other prophet before him, was being tempted to make compromises with his vocation, and that he *needed* an extraordinary grace to keep him upright. This fact throws light, one feels, on an aspect of Daniel's spiritual life which might otherwise have escaped us. In the narrative parts of the Book we see only the Prophet's unflinching purpose; in the prophetical parts we glimpse the man himself. We see him here as 'grieved,' as 'troubled,' as 'afraid,' as 'faint,' as 'confused,' as 'alone,' as wilting, one might almost say, under the demands of God. The chapters which form the body of the Prophecy— *as* prophecy—make one wish to go over the whole work again and contrast the loneliness and diffidence of the man of visions with the gaiety and decision of the man of action.

iii

Let us confine ourselves to those parts of Daniel's Book which we have been considering in these pages and, with as much of the text as we can remember—together with as much of the man as we can see—let us attempt to sum up the writer and the Book he wrote.

Just as a superficial study of Jeremias might quite easily reveal a man who is always gloomy, so a superficial study of Daniel might reveal one who is always gay. Neither view would be entirely correct. The foregoing pages have, I hope, done more than merely hint at the underlying seriousness of Daniel's spirit. But just as we are right in connecting the name of Jeremias with lamentations rather than with lampoons, so I think we are right in associating with the name of Daniel a certain *enjouement* which is hardly to be found in his fellow-prophets. A modern writer has called the Book of Daniel ' a pleasing little idyl ' ; if it is no more than that, the Bible might quite well do without it. Whatever else it is, the Book of Daniel is not *just* an ' idyl.' The work—even such parts of it as we have taken for our present study—is much too deep in feeling to find a place in ' whimsy-whamsy ' literature ; at the same time it is—let us concede this much to the modern writer—too light-hearted in treatment to rank among the Osees, the Jobs, and the Jeremiases. But if classification is absent from this summing up— and I cheerfully admit that the Book of Daniel cannot be fitted easily into any one category—at least I am prepared to come forward with criticism and conjecture. I submit accordingly (and at the risk of being pedantic) that Daniel's ' method ' was this : he avoided limiting

what might be called the ' artistry ' of his Book to any
one of the corresponding attributes in his own make-up.
And as a result you get a curiously mixed work : you
get a Book which contains comedy and tragedy, you
get at once a mystical and a practical Book, an
historical and a prophetical Book, a Book of colour
and movement and life, a Book of struggle and prayer
and death . . . a Book in which there seems to be no
order, and yet one in which the very lack of order is so
consistent as to suggest a deliberate plan. You can
pick up a thread here and a thread there, and you can
trace your thread right back from the last chapter to
the first : you can see the same moral in each of Daniel's
wonders, you can see the same temptation in each of
Babylon's kings. But the threads lie so criss-cross
upon the frame that the tapestry's design is hardly
seen.

I submit, therefore, that Daniel's craftsmanship was
conscious and even conscientious ; that the science of
the craft is all the more subtle because it was intended
to appear unconsidered ; that Daniel, who knew well
enough how to plan a plot and set a stage, deliberately
avoided a programme because he looked to the *purpose*
of the production. Such is the method, incidentally,
though not the aim, of a considerable number of writers
at the present time.[1]

Daniel, with the utmost forethought and purpose,
painted stars of gold and patches of the palest blue
where otherwise there would have appeared only
purples and olive-greens. It was Josephus, with his
historian's eye, who saw mostly the purple underneath.

---

[1] Where, however, the technique of arrangement is preferred to
the matter which is arranged ; in Daniel, on the other hand, it is
the matter which pleases, while it is the arrangement which escapes
observation.

Stevenson says somewhere (I think in a letter) that
a book must have one general tendency : that there
must not be a single word in it ' that looks the other
way.' In Daniel ' the general tendency '—as I have
tried to show from the start—is there ; but all the
words—as I am trying to show in retrospect—' look
the other way.' And because they are *meant* to, and
because they do so often enough, they help rather than
hinder ' the general tendency.' I have tried in my
own commentary (God forgive me) to follow the
example of my author. Only, of course, in my case
the words do not all look in the other direction, they
look in all directions at once.

Now if we are in any way right in our conjecture as
to the scientific lightness of Daniel's touch, there is still
the obvious question to be met—Why did he do it ?
Partly, perhaps, because he was thereby being true to
his temperament (when it would have been false to
have pursued a sombre course from cover to cover),
and partly because to say sad things cheerfully was so
absolutely necessary to the age in which he lived.
Consider that the Jews for whom he wrote were most
of them exiled, and all of them—whether at home in
Judea, or away in Egypt and Babylonia—disinherited
and dispossessed ; consider what Daniel's public had
suffered since the fall of Jerusalem : loss of fervour,
loss of hope, loss—very often—of faith ; consider the
dark expectations which, whether in Judea or Chaldea,
the future held in store ; consider the threats and woes,
which, whenever they turned the pages of the older
prophets, reproached them for their want of faith. . . .
Was Daniel wrong when he decided that his message
should be clothed in words of joy ? Surely it was a
great part of Daniel's strength that he ' continued unto

the reign of Cyrus' overlaying with the brightest gold
when everything—canvas, palette, models, artist himself sometimes—was fading into grey. The Prophet
may or may not have wanted to be out of it all,[1] but,
while he was in it, he was determined to *live ;* and,
like the prince in the fairy tale, to do so happily ever
after. We have quoted Stevenson once, let us do so
again : ' Glad did I live, and gladly die '—Stevenson's
epitaph can be suitably shared by the Prophet of
Israel.

·   ·   ·   ·   ·

' God alone can fill the vast abyss of my desires,'[2]
which is only another way of saying what another
servant of God has said already : ' I shall be satisfied
when Thy glory shall appear '[3] . . . glad now, but
satisfied hereafter.

[1] For my part, as I say, I think he *did* look forward to his death
among the lions.
[2] St Teresa of Lisieux, *Autobiography*, p. 128.
[3] Psalm xvi, 15.

BIBLIOGRAPHY

Bevan, A. A., *A Short Commentary on the Book of Daniel*, 1892.

Charles, R. H., *A Critical and Exegetical Commentary on the Book of Daniel*, 1929.

Deane, H., *Daniel, his Life and Times*, 1888.

Driver, S. R., *Daniel* (Cambridge Bible), 1936.

Duff, M., and Hope, N., *Daniel the Prophet*.

Hastings, J., *Dictionary of the Bible*, 1898.

Kelly, W., *Lectures on the Book of Daniel*.

Lods, A., *The Prophets and the Rise of Judaism*, 1937.

Marston, Sir Charles, *The Bible Comes Alive*, 1938.

Moran, T., *Introduction to Scripture*, 1937.

Pinches, T. G., *The Old Testament in the Light of the Historical Records of Assyria and Babylonia*, 1903.

Pope, H., *The Catholic Student's 'Aids' to the Bible*, Vol. II, 1930.

Pusey, E. B., *Lectures on Daniel the Prophet*, 1864.

Smith, Sir George A., *Historical Atlas of the Holy Land*, 1936.

Smith, Sir William, *Dictionary of the Bible*, 1896.

St Clair, G., *Buried Cities and Bible Countries*, 1891.

Wardle, W. L., *Israel and Babylon*, 1925.